PRAISE FOR
Ignite Your Selling Potential

"**A must-read for all sales organizations!** This is the **first sales book** that I have seen that incorporates online tools that are simple, practical, and will drive results. I strongly recommend Susan's **unique approach** to **transforming productivity into great sales results**."

—KEITH FERGUSON
Sr. Sales Director, Biogen

"What is different about the book, *Ignite Your Selling Potential*, and Susan Lund's work is that it is **practical, easy to use, and produces sustainable revenue growth and results fast. I know that first hand.**"

—SCOTT GREGORIA
Sales Leader

"*Ignite Your Selling Potential* provides a solid, **strategic roadmap that equips** and **empowers every employee to get on the same page** to **deliver differentiated value** to clients during **every interaction**. New to sales or tenured professional, you will benefit from this easy-to-read, complete guide to professional sales. Well done!"

—KAREN EKLIN
Sales Consultant

"*Ignite Your Selling Potential* is a must-read for any executive team looking to achieve alignment to focus on what it takes to grow profitable revenue. The practical strategies and principles in this book have not only benefited our sales team but have made a positive impact in other departments as well."

—Kate Broman, MBA
Vice President of Finance & Administration, MINT Roofing

"Having worked with Susan as a coach and consultant for our business and sales team, it is exciting to see her brilliance come through in a single book/system that will surely **benefit many organizations looking to get all of their teams driving in the same direction.**"

—Michele Krolczyk
Vice President of Marketing/Owner, MINT Roofing

"You don't have to be in a traditional sales profession to benefit from *Ignite Your Selling Potential.* As an attorney who counsels in-house business clients, I've found the tools in the book to be instrumental in helping me 'sell' my message to my clients. **Read the book; do the work; apply the principles. You'll be rewarded.**"

—Julie Savoie Wingert
In-house Legal Counsel

"*Ignite Your Selling Potential* is **a must-read** for any person who wants to grow personally and professionally. **Even the most tenured sales professional and sales manager can benefit from this book.** It provides innovative strategies and steps to get everyone on the same page, driving revenue and results and optimizing value to their customers. When Susan states, 'I really care about your success personally and professionally,' she REALLY means it."

—CHRISTINE ADAMSKI
Medical Sales Professional

"*Ignite Your Selling Potential* holds the possibility of guiding a business to do just that, especially as they apply what they learn. Susan Lund melds proven principles into an **impressive narrative and game plan capable of transforming your sales organization or company.**"

—LARRY SCHNEIDERMAN
CEO, Schneiderman's Furniture

"We all yearn to realize our potential, yet few actually do. Everyone is selling or unselling every day. Any individual or team or executive can **gain practical insight to realize, ignite, and maximize their selling potential** with the lessons that Susan teaches in this book."

—MARK E. DEFFNER
Attorney and Legal Technology Entrepreneur, Pauly, DeVries Smith & Deffner, L.L.C.

"You are unlikely to find a better, more practical and inspiring guide that maps principles and strategies for engaging the mind and heart to the ends of **accelerated results, maximized performance and professional fulfillment.**"

—KEN GEIS
Executive Pastor, Calvery Church

"Personally, as I used the powerful tools and coaching with *Ignite Your Selling Potential*, I gained valuable insight to what drives me, not to mention clarity on my destination. **This is for more than sales teams. It's for anyone who wants to be successful.** What I like most is being intentional about my choices and gaining clarity on where I am going."

—Patty Salmon
Senior Customer Service Manager, GNP Company

"**We all have untapped potential** and can **benefit from transforming activity into productivity to achieve results**. Susan is passionate about equipping and inspiring people and organizations to achieve their goals."

—Patricia Groziak
Executive Director, Nutrition & Wellness, Golin

"*Ignite Your Selling Potential* provides **invaluable lessons in success** for professionals at any level. It is a **must-read for anyone seeking a future as a leader, manager, or executive.**"

—Nate Paulson

"If you don't think you are a sales person, think again. Work, community, and home—everyone is selling. Immediately I could see how the *Ignite* **strategies would benefit me professionally and personally, whether working with clients or working with volunteers or fundraising.**

Ignite is more than just a good read! Susan provides a cross-functional approach with flexibility for different learning styles and situations AND gives the tools to incorporate the learning to be more successful. **I couldn't wait to take the wheel and start driving.**"

—Deb Oetjens Jackson
Business Development Manager

"*Ignite Your Selling Potential* **helps leaders address the execution gap! It provides a systematic way** for the **entire organization** to **execute** a sales strategy that drives revenue and results."

—Nancy K. Eberhardt
CEO, Pathwise Partners, and author, *Uncommon Candor: A Leader's Guide to Straight Talk*

IGNITE

YOUR SELLING

POTENTIAL

IGNITE

YOUR SELLING

POTENTIAL

7 SIMPLE
accelerators to
DRIVE REVENUE
and
RESULTS FAST

S U S A N   A .   L U N D

PRESIDENT, MR³ CONSULTING

MR³

Published by Advantage, Charleston, South Carolina.
Member of Advantage Media Group.

ADVANTAGE is a registered trademark and the Advantage colophon is a trademark of Advantage Media Group, Inc.

Printed in the United States of America.

ISBN: 978-1-59932-525-5
LCCN: 2015939363

Book design by Megan Elger.

This publication is designed to provide accurate and authoritative information in regard to the subject matter covered. It is sold with the understanding that the publisher is not engaged in rendering legal, accounting, or other professional services. If legal advice or other expert assistance is required, the services of a competent professional person should be sought.

Advantage Media Group is proud to be a part of the Tree Neutral® program. Tree Neutral offsets the number of trees consumed in the production and printing of this book by taking proactive steps such as planting trees in direct proportion to the number of trees used to print books. To learn more about Tree Neutral, please visit **www.treeneutral.com**. To learn more about Advantage's commitment to being a responsible steward of the environment, please visit **www.advantagefamily.com/green**

Advantage Media Group is a publisher of business, self-improvement, and professional development books and online learning. We help entrepreneurs, business leaders, and professionals share their Stories, Passion, and Knowledge to help others Learn & Grow. Do you have a manuscript or book idea that you would like us to consider for publishing? Please visit **advantagefamily.com** or call **1.866.775.1696.**

To my dad for inspiring me to invest my talents to help others succeed and to my mom who encouraged me to pursue my passions and told me, "You can do anything you set your mind to."

ACKNOWLEDGMENTS

I would like to say thank you to:

My husband for all of his support as I worked for hours on end to write this book and create the system to support readers with a companion website, tools, online learning, and courses, which was no small feat;

My family and friends for their encouragement;

My clients who have shared their testimonials and feedback every step of the way;

My business partners for their collaboration;

My publisher and entire team at Advantage Media Group;

My current and past colleagues;

Leaders who inspired me: Dr. John C. Maxwell, Dr. Stephen R. Covey, Jim Collins and Jack Welch, Simon Sinek, and Bill George.

After finishing this manuscript, I took a long run on the trails around Lake Minnetonka, one of Minnesota's 10,000 lakes, reflecting upon what impact this book would have on you, the reader.

After working so many hours every evening and weekend with the intent to add value to you personally and professionally, I would very much enjoy hearing the impact this book and entire system has on you and your team.

My hope is that this will inspire, equip, and empower you to apply what you learn to realize, ignite, and maximize your individual, team, and organizational selling potential. As a result, you will increase your job satisfaction and contribution to accelerate revenue, achieve results, and deliver differentiated value during every interaction, not to mention enhance your personal and professional life.

Feel free to share your feedback with me.

Susan

Susan A. Lund
susan@sellingpotential.com
www.IgniteYourSellingPotential.com
April 8th, 2015

RESULTS AND TESTIMONIALS
FOR MR³ CONSULTING

The strategies in this book have been road-tested by a wide range of companies across a variety of industries. Below are examples of results my clients have experienced utilizing the proven strategies, principles, and processes in this book and engaging MR³ Consulting, a metrics-driven sales, leadership, and productivity consulting firm.

- $169M in incremental revenue within six months

- $8B in incremental revenue within 12 months

- $12M incremental within 12 months

- $1M within one week

- $30M within six months

- $500K within two months

- $1M increase in valuation within 12 months

- $366,000 in seven months

- $250,000 in one month

Revenue generation like this means these organizations are fueling stronger relationships with their clients and creating differentiated value, not to mention having fun because revenue is coming in the door.

The industries these results represent include financial, health care, medical-device, manufacturing, professional services, technology, and nonprofit. Some include direct sales channels, and others include distributor channels.

In each case, the sales team and departments supporting sales worked in alignment with my firm to *ignite the selling potential* within their organization.

TESTIMONIALS

"As a VP of marketing and sales, I have found that the collaboration and partnership with Susan Lund and MR³ has been instrumental to the success of each of our sales teams. It has been powerful to see the changes in my sales leadership team. Having a common language and framework to drive execution and achieve results is essential to the success of any sales leadership team. This same common framework and vision was also used to drive alignment and execution with our marketing, training, and business partners. **I have enjoyed working with Susan Lund and appreciate how she has raised the bar with our sales leadership and sales teams.** As a result, both my team and I have referred her and her firm to multiple leaders within our organization. I would **highly recommend her and her company** to any VPs of sales and marketing or senior executives **who want to grow their sales, strengthen their sales management team, and build a high performance sales culture to optimize their customer experience.**"

—**Dean Ferkinhoff**
Vice President of Marketing and Sales

"As a divisional vice president of sales, I have found the collaboration and partnership with Susan Lund and MR³ has been instrumental to the successful integration and development of our sales teams. It has been rewarding to experience the high adoption rate and buy-in from my team to continually improve their selling skills. **What's different about MR³ is Susan's leadership skills, thoroughness, and ability to help the leaders and sales professionals succeed.** Having a common language and framework to drive execution and achieve results is essential to the success of any sales leadership and sales team.

—**DREW DISHER**
Divisional Vice President of Sales

"I have had the opportunity to work very closely with Susan at a large medical company. She was in charge of launching an entire new program to the sales force that would take our sales to a new level. And to a new level VERY quickly, if we followed Susan's formula for success. **Her outstanding leadership and interpersonal skills instantly created buy-in from the sales force and helped us immediately achieve aggressive sales growth.** She is always looking for ways to create a win-win-win situation for everyone.

Susan freely shares her gifts with others so they may succeed. She is a lifetime coach who is always there for you. She listens very intently and then formulates, presents, and coaches a person throughout the implementation process so they may obtain quick success.

There is only one way Susan conducts business, which is with high integrity. Any company will have the peace of mind that they are truly working with a top-notch, ethical person. **If you want to achieve aggressive sales growth and help your team succeed, I highly recommend you have Susan as part of your plan.**"

—**CHRISTINE ADAMSKI**
Sales Manager

"Susan does a magnificent job of bringing both common sense and practical business goals into her sales training initiatives. Her ability to focus on achieving sales force efficiency and productivity in an accelerated timeline produces tangible and early results."

—DAVID HARBECK

General Counsel of a leading health-care company

"**In three months we more than doubled our pipeline, from $49M to $106M, on one product, and tripled it on another product, from $3.2M to $9M. Our pipeline has grown to $140M plus**. Our team has closed over $12M in revenue for the six months of our new fiscal year. We are in a much better place this year after working with MR³ than previously. As a CEO of an emerging growth company, **I hired MR³, a metrics-driven sales productivity consulting firm to help us navigate through a critical juncture**. We needed to pivot quickly and figure out how to gain access to more capital and grow our sales. We needed an outside strategic perspective to identify what was holding us back from growing our sales. Once we could identify what was missing, we were able to address the issues. I have more confidence in knowing what is needed to grow our sales. Now it is all about execution of our plan. In addition, I have hired Susan as an executive coach. I would recommend her to any CEOs who want to grow their company's sales or increase their productivity."

—FRANK ALTMAN

President and CEO of Community Reinvestment Fund, USA

"I met Susan Lund with MR³, a metrics-driven sales and productivity consulting firm, when she spoke at our CEO group a year ago. We had inconsistent peaks and valleys of sales and profitability. **Susan has literally transformed our sales team from a reactive team to a highly engaged successful team. Our sales and profit continue to grow.** She is well respected by the entire sales and management team. Her follow-up is exceptional. I have learned to raise my bar. **Not only have we produced profitable results in four short months, we now have a process in place to repeat profitable revenue growth.** Every senior executive who wants to grow their sales profitably can benefit from getting to know and work with Susan Lund."

—KEVIN KROLCZYK
President and Owner, Mint Roofing

"Personally, as a sales leader, I have enjoyed the partnership with Susan Lund, President of MR³ Consulting. She has been well received by our sales team and sales directors. She continually anticipates what is needed to help our team succeed in achieving results. I would highly recommend her and her company for any company that wants to grow its sales."

—AARON J. GORDON
Vice President of Sales

"**MR³'s work has been powerful for our team, our customers, and our company. If you want consistent, repeatable results, profitability, and sales growth, I would highly recommend MR³, a metrics-drive sales and productivity consulting firm.** I would recommend her to any executives who want to grow sales, develop a high performance sales culture, and optimize their customer experience."

—CHAD CARSON
President

"What is different about Susan is that she practices what she teaches. **Interacting with Susan is a lesson in leadership**. I would highly recommend Susan Lund as a coach to any executive because I know her coaching works."

—MICHAEL ERB
Vice President of Marketing

"As VP of Development, responsible for fundraising at CRF, I have had the opportunity to work with Susan Lund, President of MR³ Consulting. As a result of our work together, **I exceeded my fundraising goal for the year by achieving 108 percent of plan**. I would recommend Susan Lund and MR³ to any executives or organizations who want to grow their sales."

—WARREN McLEAN
Vice President of Development

"We have engaged Susan Lund on a variety of specific engagements. **As CFO, I'm particularly interested in the value she brings**. Unlike many other consultants, I feel she brings to bear immediate and proven tools to solve problems and make firms like CRF more effective. I strongly recommend Susan."

—SCOTT YOUNG
Senior Vice President and Chief Financial Officer

Table of Contents

Focused Goals and Action Plans + Consistent Daily
Action = Predictable Repeatable Results

*How important is it to have access to a proven formula that
works?*

PHASE III: FOCUS

Time + Pipeline Management + Focus = Sustainable
Results

*What 20 percent of your activities produce 80 percent of
results?*

Visibility + Metrics + Accountability = Accelerated
Performance

What are you accountable for?

Value + Differentiation = Choice

*How much differentiated value do your clients perceive
when you present your solution?*

*A Roadmap for Individual, Team, and Organization
Acceleration*

INTRODUCTION

"This is the most engaged team I have ever seen."

*"One thing that makes the training unique is the
ability for your learners to apply their training
to life skills, not just product sales."*

"I wish I had this when I started with this company."

*"As a sales director, now I understand why it is important
to have a common framework for my entire team."*

These unsolicited quotes from the president of a Fortune 500 company, a sales consultant, and a sales director, respectively, encourage me every day to dedicate my time to help individuals, teams, and organizations ignite their selling potential to drive results fast.

They were made at a time I will never forget. I had just finished implementing one of our sales productivity solutions for a new sales team, sales director, and business unit. One month after training, the president came to inspect the progress the team was making and made the remark that he had never seen any team so engaged.

What those individuals learned is that having a common roadmap and consistent language made it much easier to do their job and perform. Not having a common roadmap and tools makes it challenging. New team members come in with different languages, processes, and tools that create roadblocks for performance. Not having a common language leaves the new hires and manager speaking different languages. But as this team adopted a common language, roadmap, and necessary tools, they were able to navigate around these challenges and focus on gaining a fast start.

This was a significant change in how new hires were brought into the organization. Before this, their time to productivity was longer because they didn't have a roadmap, let alone one built for speed. They were simply provided with their customer list, basic tools such as a computer and phone, and told to go sell. Sound familiar? Now their bar had been raised. They knew how much more successful everyone could be when they had a roadmap built for speed.

You too will find the carryover of benefits in your personal life as you apply the principles in *Ignite Your Selling Potential*. They impact every relationship and interaction you have or will have in the future. When people are at a critical juncture or crossroad, uncertain of which way to turn, I am passionate about helping them succeed.

And there's more. This team produced $169M in incremental revenue within six months. The vice president of sales and sales director were so pleased with the results that they asked me to partner with them to launch another new business unit and team. One year later, our second team produced $8B in incremental revenue. Five years later, these businesses are significant revenue-generating engines for the entire company.

This is but one example of the success that the guidance in this book can bring to you, and there are many other examples of existing teams that have made significant gains from our work together. Another team achieved a 20-year high in sales and said there was no way they could have done this without me and my processes.

It's gratifying to see how sales professionals, teams, and organizations benefit from gaining a fast start and achieving results with my proven processes. I have always believed that if you give sales professionals what they need, they will sell more faster. The key is to give them what they need to ignite their potential and achieve the desired results. By also igniting the entire team's potential, together you can build a high-performing team focused on understanding your clients' needs, delivering differentiated value, and optimizing the client experience.

What you are about to read is the culmination of 30 years of strategies, skills, and proven principles that work to ignite selling potential and drive results fast. For 20 years I have taught these principles and listened to sales professionals, sales managers, and CEOs tell me how much more effective their teams have been in accelerating revenue, achieving results, and fueling strong relationships with their customers. They have become much more confident as they have ignited their selling potential. It is with great joy that I share these strategies, skills, and proven principles with you.

A CAREER DEDICATED TO ACCELERATING SALES AND DELIVERING VALUE

I learned early in my career the value of giving sales professionals what they need to succeed. I started my career with General Mills and was quickly promoted to its emerging growth division, launching Yoplait USA, a yogurt company, in the United States. After consistently exceeding my sales quota and driving results fast, I was recruited by a division of another world-class company,

Codman Shurtleff, an emerging growth division of Johnson and Johnson. As I crossed the chasm from selling in the grocery stores to the operating room, standing on three stepstools over Dr. Denton Cooley's shoulders as he performed multiple open-heart surgeries a day, I experienced the benefit of high-performance training, culture, and leadership. This would never have been possible if I hadn't had what I needed to ignite my own selling potential to grow the business.

I was responsible for growing over ten franchises in the world's renowned medical center in Houston, Texas, and southern Texas. It was an awesome responsibility, one in which I needed to know my products inside and out so I could literally teach and sell in the OR to physicians using the instruments to treat patients and save lives. It was at J & J that I learned from the best mentors, the best managers, and the best trainers. That is where I learned about excellence. As a result, I won numerous awards and was asked to train new hires.

What I learned about myself during this time was that it was more fun helping others succeed and win awards than it was to win them myself. That pattern of consistently accelerated sales and winning continued throughout my career fueled by the purpose to deliver value to customers and help other sales professionals and teams succeed.

Everywhere I go, I assess revenue generation and value to the customer. As I scaled sales from $5M to $139M in less than three years and contributed to doubling the revenue of our company from $200M to $450M in 2.5 years, various people began asking me to mentor, train, and coach them. When I did, they succeeded.

More than 300,000 sales professionals, sales leaders, and organizations have experienced results by applying my principles to accelerate sales. Fortune 500 companies, most kept confidential due to the competitive nature of the marketplace, along with mid- to small-sized businesses both public and privately held, have experienced results from the fundamentals in this book. Several are as follows: Community Reinvestment Fund USA, Thomson Reuters, General Mills, Johnson and Johnson, and Schering Plough Oncology Biotech.

WHY I WROTE THIS BOOK

I felt compelled to write this book after finding so many people didn't have what they needed to succeed, achieve their goals, or get to their destination on time. They continued to run into hazards, go off-road, and not know how to navigate around them. I felt for them. They were in a tough situation. Thus, I found myself asking, "How can I help?"

I want to help by providing you with a strategic roadmap with specific strategies, principles, and tools so that, regardless of your challenges and where you are when you start this book, you will learn what hazards to avoid, how to navigate to your destination, and what you can do to an individual, team, and organization to achieve results. Doing so will help you develop long-term relationships and have fun selling.

Selling is an individual, team, and organizational sport. The more people and departments within the company who are aligned around creating differentiated value and helping the customers succeed, the more successful the organization will be. It's critical to a sales professional's success to have a sales culture and sales manager who reinforce, reward, and coach based on this predefined set of strategies and fundamentals on a consistent basis.

Engaged individuals and teams create engaged customers. With a practical roadmap to ignite your potential, you can accelerate revenue and drive results fast. You are in the driver's seat!

Successful sales organizations that consistently meet or exceed their revenue targets are focused on helping their sales professionals succeed. Successful leaders view their people—not their products, services, or company—as their greatest asset.

The good news is that regardless of your role, you can accelerate revenue, achieve results, and fuel stronger relationships if you have a practical roadmap to ignite your potential and transform activity into productivity®. Within 90 days, you too can ignite your selling potential and experience greater job satisfaction, compress time to productivity, and experience more success.

> *"Personal development is the belief that you are worth the effort, time, and energy needed to develop yourself."*
>
> —DENIS WAITLEY

HOW TO REALIZE AND MAXIMIZE YOUR POTENTIAL

You will get the most out of this book when you:

- Take the assessment to gain visibility of your untapped selling potential and know your score. You can access the assessment at www.IgniteYourSellingPotential.com.

- Utilize the action items, application questions, and exercises at the end of each chapter. You and your sales team can immediately apply these to accelerate your sales.

- Take action to apply what you learn within the next 90 days. Doing so will enable you to ignite your selling potential.

If you are a manager and want to help your team succeed, consider reviewing a chapter a week, discussing your answers as a team, and applying what you've learned within the next 90 days. The best way to use this book is to go through it from start to finish as a team, sharing your thoughts and experiences, using the strategies with your team.

For faster results, there are additional resources such as powerful productivity tools and online learning at the end of each chapter along with courses for acceleration at the back of the book.

As you start your journey, I want you to know that I care about your success personally and professionally, know how to help you succeed, and believe in you! You are your company's greatest asset—so buckle your seatbelt and put your hands on the wheel, you are in the driver's seat. Let's get started!

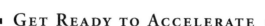
I often compare selling to driving a car: most people do it every day, yet it is easy to get distracted with activity. It's the same with selling. If you are communicating with internal customers or external customers, you are either selling, being outsold, or unselling during every interaction, every day.

Due to the rapid pace of the marketplace and the rate at which technology is revolutionizing every industry, the need to transform how we think and compete is critical to gaining a competitive advantage and growing revenue.

The difference between people who consistently drive performance and people who don't is in how well they prepare, plan, and focus on what they need to do to hit their goals. Those three critical pieces—prepare, plan, and focus—make up the three sections of this book. Within them, you will learn about the 7 Accelerators™ that will put you on the fast track to driving revenue and results. These 7 Accelerators™ will put you in the driver's seat and give you the power to choose to Transform Activity Into Productivity®.

> *"The illiterate of the 21st century will not be those who cannot read and write, but those who cannot learn, unlearn, and relearn."*
>
> **—ALVIN TOFFLER, FUTURIST**

It sounds simple enough, but it's easy to get sidetracked. The reality is, when you don't prepare, plan, and focus, you wind up spinning your wheels and leaving potential sales on the side of the road. When you do take charge and ignite your selling potential, you will realize and maximize your job satisfaction and contribution. The good news is that regardless of your role—whether you are new to sales, a seasoned team leader, or an executive—you have untapped selling potential. Realizing, igniting, and maximizing your selling potential will help you become more successful.

WHAT IS *SALES*?

Let's start by agreeing on the definition of sales. When I ask people to finish the sentence, "*Sales* is ..." it's interesting to hear their responses. They will say things such as:

> *Sales is ... all about relationships.*

> *Sales is ... about making the number.*

> *Sales is ... a numbers game. The more*
> *people you contact the better.*

If sales is all about relationships, then how do you generate revenue? If sales is all about the number, then it excludes delivering value to the customer.

The problem with *sales* being a numbers game where the more people you contact, the better, is that more activity doesn't necessarily produce better results and can, in fact, be a waste of time. Furthermore, it consumes more resources, thus increasing the cost of sales and decreasing profitability.

The reality is that *sales* doesn't mean just one thing. It is a combination of the right activities done for the right reason to produce a result.

To me, *sales* means acting as a trusted partner to gain agreement and choose your solutions *instead of the competition's* to solve unmet needs. *Sales* is about the value exchange, value creation, and differentiation from the competition. It is about empowering your customers to choose the best solutions to solve their unmet needs. The true test of successful selling is whether your customer chooses you instead of the competition. Selling = Influence. Leadership also equals Influence. The true test of a leader is whether people choose to follow you. Leaders gain followership by understanding peoples' needs and creating value to help their people, company, and team succeed.

> *Sales means acting as a trusted partner to gain agreement and choose your solutions instead of the competition's to solve unmet needs. Sales is about the value exchange, value creation, and differentiation from the competition.*

Selling is simply planned communication to create differentiated value, empowering your customers to choose the best solution to solve their unmet needs. When you prepare, plan, and focus, you can ignite more of your selling potential. Doing so will enable you to consistently

> *Selling = Influence. Leadership also equals Influence.*

discover and agree on the unmet needs to deliver differentiated value to your customers.

> *The true test of successful selling is whether your customer chooses you instead of the competition.*

The difference between top performers and the rest is that the top performers prepare, plan, and focus on the right things that drive revenue and achieve results. At the same time, they avoid the negative consequences of not doing so. Therefore, the customer will choose to buy from them instead of the competition. Those who are successful learn how to do this exceptionally well.

Depending on whether you have direct or indirect responsibility for revenue, everyone is selling. While you may not have a formal role in selling, the ability to sell is very important. In addition, everyone is responsible for results. Let's explore the types of selling situations by role so you can see how improving your selling potential can personally help you succeed. Circle those that apply to you.

ROLE	SELLING SITUATIONS	COMMON SALES CHALLENGES
Sales Professional	Scheduling a meeting with a prospect	Customers don't call back. Tough to gain access.
Sales Professional	Selling to executive teams or multiple people involved in making a decision	Gaining buy-in from everyone.
Sales Professional	Presenting the solution	Customers don't see value or appreciate the difference. Your solution is perceived as a commodity.

ROLE	SELLING SITUATIONS	COMMON SALES CHALLENGES
Sales Professional	Competitive bidding	Customers always go with the lowest bid or price. They don't see enough value.
Marketing	Sales support or sales enablement	Lack of follow through on marketing initiatives; programs, messaging, branding, etc. Tough to gain support to approve marketing materials.
Marketing	Understanding what sales needs	When I ask them, they always tell me they want more. However, they are not using what they have.
Manager	Execution	Tough to get buy-in and execution for specific actions to achieve results. Employees are not doing what you want them to do to execute.
Manager	Cross functional partner support or buy-in	Lack of support or buy-in.

As you can see, it doesn't matter what your role is. If you are communicating, you are always selling, unselling, or being outsold. Other roles and situations involved in selling include the following:

- Human resources professionals need to sell potential hires on why they should join their company.

- Sales managers need to sell to gain access to resources for their team.

- Employees, when talking with a friend or acquaintance, need to have a compelling statement about what their company does and the value it delivers in order to generate referrals to the sales team or potential employees who may want to work at the company.

- The CEO and CFO need to sell to the board or investors.

Your ability to ignite your selling potential is essential to gaining buy-in, which is essential to getting your work done. Whether you are an executive leading a team, a manager with direct reports or cross-functional partners, or a sales professional, the question is, "Is your customer choosing you and your solution, idea, recommendation, product, or service instead of the competition?" In other words, are they buying? For managers, the question is, "Are your people following you? Are they buying into your direction? What value have you created for them?"

WHAT IS ACCELERATION ANYWAY?

Acceleration is at the intersection of three corners: preparation, strategic planning, and focus. People who arrive at their destination on time

- consistently drive revenue and results and fuel strong relationships;
- continually strive to realize, ignite, and maximize their potential to increase their productivity and consistently deliver differentiated value to customers with on-time arrival at their destination;

> *Acceleration is at the intersection of three corners: preparation, strategic planning, and focus.*

- outpace those who don't, thus arriving there faster!

You see these kinds of behaviors in companies that

are thriving today. Examples include Cargill, the largest privately held company in the world; Apple Inc., which has become the dominant player and market leader; and Under Armour, which continues to expand its market presence and brand and establish its leadership position. Individuals, teams, and organizations that consistently do these things well create markets, dominate industries, and become unstoppable forces to be reckoned with.

WHAT SUCCESS LOOKS LIKE

Minnesota is the home of the number-one privately held company in the world, Cargill. One of the reasons Cargill has been so successful year after year is because of its ability to have clarity on structure, roles, expectations, and destination. The leaders do an exceptional job of not only strategic planning one and five years out but also ten-plus years out. The company dominates the market by creating the market and establishing market leadership. The company also gains a competitive advantage by getting ahead of the competition, strategically. Cargill invests heavily in its people and understands the relationship between developing people and driving performance. Cargill makes intentional strategic choices about how to continue to deliver value to customers. There is a lot to learn from this.

It's a lot like using a GPS. You have to enter a destination in the device before it can determine a route to get there. Why is this important? Peak performance requires clarity on the desired destination and a predefined sequence. The same applies for driving revenue and results and fueling long-term relationships.

PHASE I

PREPARE

SLOW DOWN TO SPEED UP

AWARENESS + PERSONAL NAVIGATION = IGNITE
POTENTIAL

*There are two primary choices in life: to accept conditions as
they exist, or accept the responsibility for changing them.*

—**DENIS WAITLEY**

Nobody starts off fast. Although it seems counterintuitive, the
first step to speeding up your sales acceleration is slowing down.

Sales professionals, managers, and executives sometimes
think it's the customers' fault when they can't see the value in the
solutions or ideas in front of them. But the real reason customers
don't see value is oftentimes because the person selling has not
created value. You see, if we are not getting the result we want,
sometimes we need to look in the mirror and ask, "What can I do
differently?" Or we need to seek the counsel of a friend or mentor
whom we trust to ask, "What am I missing? What are my blind

spots?" One of my favorite authors and mentors is John Maxwell, and he says, **"Blind spots are areas in which people continually fail to see themselves or their situation realistically."**

We all have blind spots because we see our actions as a result of our intentions. However, others don't know our intentions unless we communicate them. Thus, others respond to our actions.

Because of that, instead of jumping right in with a sales presentation, it's important to slow down and reflect. You can do this by following two simple steps for acceleration: 1) know your score, and 2) ignite your selling potential.

STEP 1: KNOW YOUR SCORE

Hidden inside you is untapped selling potential that has not been discovered or fully developed.

Realizing your potential is the culmination of beliefs, thoughts, capacity, gifts, strengths, and actions working together in alignment toward a purpose and vision that is bigger than you. In this book, we will focus on your selling potential. As you ignite it, you will be able to create differentiated value for your customers during each interaction and sell more faster. You will also be able to identify and release the activities at the end of each chapter that are holding you back from achieving your goals. Next, you will be able to take action to apply what you learn to experience success.

Prior to realizing your potential, you will yearn for greater satisfaction, enjoyment, and fulfillment in your personal and professional lives. We all do. Have you ever asked any of these questions?

- How do I find my sweet spot?

- Am I in my strength zone? What do I really want to do?

- Should I make a career or job change?

- Does what I do matter?

- How do I find my passion?

- What is the purpose of my life?

Success is an inside job before it becomes visible on the outside. Align your deepest passions with your core values, purpose, and vision. Igniting your selling potential is also an inside job. Successful people work to gain clarity about those questions and more. You are in the driver's seat, and that is why this book is tailored to you. When you learn what drives you and how to channel your gifts, strengths, and ability to ignite your selling potential, you will achieve greater satisfaction and results than ever before.

> *Success is an inside job before it becomes visible on the outside.*

Knowing how much untapped selling potential you have helps you know where to start to ignite your selling potential, so you can accelerate your sales. What percentage of your potential are you really using on a daily basis in the workplace? You will soon find out by taking a personal assessment.

Assessments can reveal our blind spots and opportunities for growth. On my website, www.IgniteYourSellingPotential.com, you will be able to gain access to an assessment that will help you identify the things you are doing well and the things you could be doing better. Taking this assessment will help you identify and develop your strengths, identify opportunities for growth, and ignite your selling potential.

Taking this assessment is the first step for individuals, teams, and organizations because it will increase awareness, which is essential for growth. After taking it, you will have the power to choose where you want to start and which accelerators will be most valuable for your individual development, team development, and organization's development.

PERSONAL ASSESSMENT

Go to www.IgniteYourSellingPotential.com to take a personal assessment of how much selling potential you are currently using. Individuals and teams can then *raise their bar* by going through each accelerator step by step. If you are a new hire to the sales organization, you can gain a *FAST START* by using this as your 90-day roadmap to accelerating revenue, achieving results, and fueling stronger relationships.

HOW CAN YOU BECOME A QUADRANT 1 REVENUE GENERATOR?

As you can see by the four quadrants listed on the next page, the goal is to ignite, realize, and maximize your selling potential by applying what you learn in this book to become a Quadrant 1 revenue generator. Anyone can generate revenue and results some of the time. The key is to consistently apply these principals on a daily basis to create repeatable and predictable results.

HOW CAN YOU BECOME A REVENUE GENERATOR?

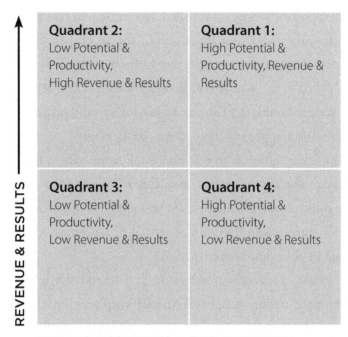

Quadrant 2:
Low Potential &
Productivity,
High Revenue & Results

Quadrant 1:
High Potential &
Productivity, Revenue &
Results

Quadrant 3:
Low Potential &
Productivity,
Low Revenue & Results

Quadrant 4:
High Potential &
Productivity,
Low Revenue & Results

REVENUE & RESULTS

SELLING POTENTIAL & PRODUCTIVITY ⟶

WHAT TO DO WITH YOUR SCORE

Once you have taken your assessment and have received your selling potential score, you may ask yourself, "What do I do now?" Knowing what to *do* with your selling potential score will help you become stronger and more successful when you sell. You'll begin to pinpoint the best way to ignite your potential to accelerate your sales, achieve results, and increase your productivity. You'll gain visibility to areas of opportunity and specific actions you can take to gain a sales edge and competitive advantage. Then, as you realize your selling potential, you will ignite and maximize your selling potential.

There are a couple ways to use your score to get started. One way is to identify the areas where you want to improve your score and then go to the step, also called accelerator, in this book that will help you strengthen those areas. The second is to identify your strengths and build upon them. There is flexibility for you to decide. After all, you are in the driver's seat. If you are like me, I read several books at a time and look for specific principles and strategies I can apply quickly—thus, like flexibility.

The other option is to read this book from start to finish and go through the steps in a sequence. This will give you an opportunity to build a solid foundation. As you apply what you learn, you can realize and maximize your potential to accelerate results and navigate to your desired destination.

Review the accelerators where you scored the lowest and develop your action plan with special emphasis on the strategies, principles, and practices at the end of each chapter for acceleration. This is something you should do not just once but regularly. I recommend that you take the assessment quarterly and then have annual tune-ups. This is the best way to realize and maximize your potential.

> *I recommend that you take the assessment quarterly and then have annual tune-ups. This is the best way to realize and maximize your potential.*

Taking a hard look at areas where you could improve can be daunting. If you are unsure whether you want to work hard to reach your potential, ask yourself,

- Will I be satisfied leaving my potential, gifts, and strengths on the side of the road and wondering what if...?

- If I had used my talents, gifts, and potential, where would I be today?

- Will I be satisfied not doing what I love or finding my true north, purpose, and vision?

- How will not reaching my potential impact my family and friends?

Early on in my career, my mentor, Larry, told me to develop a deep well of knowledge and experience before assuming additional people responsibility. Why is that important? So you have a deep well to draw from. You want to drink before you are thirsty. He and I worked together at General Mills at the time when I was promoted to the fast growth engine of the company to launch Yoplait USA, a yogurt company in the United States. From that point forward, I made development a priority. I created an

> *For businesses to grow, people need to grow.*

individual development plan. I was 130 percent to plan. My development plan and continuous learning have made a significant difference in my individual performance, my teams' performance, and my contribution to my employers. Now I share my passion for the importance of development planning with the teams I work with today. For businesses to grow, people need to grow.

As you embark upon your journey, I encourage you to take the knowledge you learn

> *One needs to take action to gain traction.*

and apply it to achieve your desired results. **One needs to take action to gain traction.** Reread that sentence; say it out loud. I have always strived to remember its meaning and truly want you to remember it as well. With your assessment in hand, you will have the power to choose where you want to start to achieve your desired goals.

> *"We almost have to force or drive ourselves to work hard if we are to reach our potential. If we don't enjoy what we do, we won't be able to push as hard as we need to push for as long as we need to push to achieve our best. However, if we enjoy what we do and if we're enthusiastic about it, we'll do it better and come closer to becoming the best we can be."*
>
> **—JOHN WOODEN**

STEP 2: IGNITE YOUR SELLING POTENTIAL

The number-one factor in success is not talent or wealth; it's personal growth. The most successful business people, athletes, and sales professionals are those who build upon their gifts and strengths and maximize their potential. In doing so, they achieve near-perfect performance every time. In fact, they have so much job satisfaction and life satisfaction that the lines between work and play blur. When you enjoy what you do, you want to do it more.

Revenue generation affects everything we do. It impacts our choices and options in life. Our career options, children's college education, retirement, health care, family, ability to add value to others, and the success or failure of our company—

nothing happens without revenue generation and results. It's the currency for choice and options.

Fast results are especially important for new hires—and teams who want to gain a competitive advantage and meet or exceed their goals. This is equally important for people who are navigating challenges and need results fast. Think about a tough spot you are in for which you need revenue and results fast. If you are in a tough spot and have gone off-road—from highway to the shoulder or in some cases the ditch—and are frustrated, do you want to get back on the road slowly or quickly? If I had gone off-road, I would want to get back on the superhighway and get to my destination fast. People who are in a tough spot and want to compress time to productivity can do so by applying the proven strategies found in this book!

It's frustrating trying to get to one's destination and not

> *Revenue generation affects everything we do. It impacts our choices and options in life. Our career options, children's college education, retirement, health care, family, ability to add value to others, and the success or failure of our company—nothing happens without revenue generation and results. It's the currency for choice and options.*

knowing how. The time to learn how to do something successfully is before you do it. As Stephen Covey says, "Highly successful people are proactive verses reactive."

RULES OF THE ROAD

Success is a choice. Successful people think differently and choose differently. The following 7 Rules of the Road will help you succeed. By using them, you will be on the superhighway to realizing and maximizing your selling potential to sell more faster.

Successful sales professionals know and practice the rules of the road. People who don't, go off-road.

---

7 RULES OF THE ROAD TO IGNITE YOUR POTENTIAL

1. Care about your customers and focus on helping them succeed.

2. Do what you say you are going to do.

3. Gain clarity to think, expect, and visualize success.

4. Prepare, plan, and practice to succeed.

5. Be humble and stay hungry.

6. Focus, focus, focus on uncovering needs, delivering differentiated value, and driving results during every interaction.

7. Arrive at your destination on time every time.

RULE #1: CARE ABOUT YOUR CUSTOMER AND FOCUS ON HELPING THEM SUCCEED

Your clients, customers, colleagues, and business partners will ask themselves several questions when they meet you. **Does this person care about me as an individual? Can she help me? Does she like me?** If they can't answer yes to all three questions, they aren't likely to buy into you. It's that simple.

I do a lot of sales training and coaching, and one of the things I have observed is that executives, managers, and sales professionals who aren't number one often start conversations by leading with their product, service, or solution pitch. They don't put the other person first. That prevents them from succeeding. The people they are selling to don't buy in! The most successful professionals care about other people, strive to help them, and like them. Managers who are successful put others' needs first. These leaders end up gaining followership because they care. To succeed, care and focus everything you do on helping your customer succeed.

RULE #2: DO WHAT YOU SAY YOU ARE GOING TO DO

Integrity means you walk the talk by doing what you say you're going to do. I remember when I was in medical sales for a small company and had 90–95 percent market share. My competitor was working hard to take my market share, which was challenging because my company was not coming out with new products anytime soon. It was difficult to increase my sales or market share because I didn't have anything new to sell whereas my competition went into my accounts with new innovative products. In an effort to protect my business, I decided to survey my customers to find out what was important to them. I was surprised to learn that the number-one thing they looked for in a sales professional was integrity.

When I learned this, I was 28 and a bit naïve because I thought everyone had integrity. I thought everyone would do what they said they were going to do. When I asked my customers to explain why integrity was the number-one thing, they replied, "Do you know how many people walk through these doors and say they are going to do something and never do?" Their answer to their own question was 99 percent of people! The takeaway is that a little integrity goes a long way. If you want to succeed, make sure your actions follow your words.

RULE #3: GAIN CLARITY TO THINK, EXPECT, AND VISUALIZE SUCCESS

> *"It comes down to something really simple: Can I visualize myself playing those scenes? If that happens, then I know that I will probably end up doing it."*
>
> **—JESSICA LANGE**

To be successful, one needs to first define what success means. The reality is that nobody achieves success without thinking it first! Visualizing and expecting success will increase your chances of achieving success.

Years ago, friends I coached really wanted me to run a marathon with them. After telling them for three years I didn't think I could, they stopped asking and told me they were going to sign me up. As I began training, I was convinced I couldn't run a marathon. It was during my longest run at the time (16 miles), as I was running up a hill with two friends, trying to catch my breath as we were having a conversation, that I said aloud, "I don't think I can run a marathon." They laughed at me and said, "You are!" That was a turning point for me. I remembered my favorite quote

> *"Whatever your mind can conceive and can believe, it can achieve."*
>
> **—NAPOLEON HILL**

as I was training to run further and faster: Henry Ford said, "Whether you think you can or think you can't, either way you are right!"

RULE #4: PREPARE, PLAN, AND PRACTICE TO SUCCEED

> *"Whether you think you can or think you can't, either way you are right!"*
>
> —HENRY FORD

We have all heard the saying, "If you fail to plan, you plan to fail." I encourage you to take that one step further. Don't just plan; plan to succeed. An unplanned conversation is an unproductive conversation. Conversations and meetings that don't have outcomes or next steps consume valuable resources and don't achieve results. They waste your customers' time and your time.

How many times have you walked out of a meeting that didn't go as well as you wanted it to and thought, "I could have been more prepared"? If we are really honest with ourselves, we can all recall a time, or more than one time, when this happened. Preparation is the hallmark of leadership. To be prepared, you have to practice, practice, practice. As John Wooden says, "How you practice is how you play." Preparation and practice are what differentiates average-performing teams from top-performing teams. Striving for excellence is a choice successful people make every day.

> *"Don't mistake activity with achievement."*
>
> —JOHN WOODEN

RULE #5: BE HUMBLE AND STAY HUNGRY

Listen and learn every day. Successful people listen more than they speak. It's hard to get to know others and their needs when you are the smartest person in the room. That dynamic stifles everyone else's potential. Successful people amplify the contributions of others. Don't act like a know-it-all. Be humble and stay hungry.

I have learned so much from listening to humble leaders. People who gain followership and buy-in learn with their customers and employees. Trust is earned by listening. Something I love to do is to build people up and amplify their contributions. Early in my career, I felt I needed to have all the answers. As I matured as a sales leader and a leader of leaders, I realized I didn't need to know all the answers and demonstrate my competency but needed to seek out people smarter than I was and learn from them. Even if I have the answer, I strive to learn something new every day. Regardless of how much you know and how successful you are, stay hungry.

RULE #6: FOCUS, FOCUS, FOCUS ON UNCOVERING UNMET NEEDS, DELIVERING DIFFERENTIATED VALUE, AND DRIVING RESULTS DURING EVERY INTERACTION

Successful people are laser focused on uncovering and understanding customers' needs and delivering value to help them achieve results. They avoid detours that distract from top priorities. Stay focused and stay on the superhighway!

> *Stay focused and stay on the superhighway!*

RULE #7: ARRIVE AT YOUR DESTINATION ON TIME EVERY TIME

Successful people consistently arrive at their destination on time or early. The top performers prepare, plan, and focus. When I think of focus, I think of a camera-like ability to zoom in and out, whenever needed, to achieve your desired results.

This book is full of strategies. I love strategy because it serves as the **superhighway to get you to your destination fast and on time.** This book and system is a superhighway to help individuals, teams, and organizations get to their destination fast. Think of me as your personal navigator, sitting side by side in the car with you to help you navigate through challenges and avoid hazards so you can confidently achieve your desired results.

AVOIDING HAZARDS

The reality is that we all go off-road and spin our wheels at times. Sometimes, we get stuck, which can feel overwhelming and become costly. The good news is that after reading this book, if you go off-road and experience a detour, you will know how to get back on the road to arrive at your destination on time. In an effort to prevent you from going off-road, I will share hazards to avoid.

In the early '90s, I took a business course and learned about engagement. When I learned about the hazard of disengagement, I decided I wanted to avoid it. According to research, organizations have not been able to solve low engagement, which has been a persistent problem for more than a decade.

Low workplace engagement offers opportunities to improve business outcomes. According to a 2013 Gallup study, only 29 percent of sales employees and 36 percent of executives, managers, and officials are engaged in their work in the USA, and the research also indicated that managers are not getting the fundamentals of performance right. There is a proven strong relationship between employees' workplace engagement and their overall performance. To avoid this hazard, I began learning about my strengths and put them to work. When I took a sales management position a short time later, I had every one of my team members learn about their strengths. I worked hard every week to build a culture of engagement that was built on the strengths of my team members. This was a stepping-stone to achieving our performance goal of growing our business 650 percent in one year. Avoiding hazards is very worthwhile!

In this section, I will share with you the hazards that can impede performance so you can avoid them. If we anticipate obstacles others have faced, we can steer around them. If we have activities that don't help us get to our goal, we can release them. I also want to caution you, when you do something every day, it's easy to go into autopilot and stop assessing, asking for feedback, and focusing on what matters most. We all have blind spots. That is why it's so important to get a quarterly tune-up and take an annual assessment to become aware of our opportunities to ignite our potential so we don't leave it on the side of the road.

> *Know Your Score:*
> *High Performers*
> *anticipate hazards*
> *BEFORE they happen*
> *so they can avoid them.*

TOP 7 HAZARDS TO AVOID AS YOU ACCELERATE YOUR SELLING POTENTIAL

1. Blind spots

2. Activity trap

3. Winging it and cruise control

4. Entitlement

5. Being the expert

6. Lack of belief in self or others

7. Wrong metrics

HAZARD #1: BLIND SPOTS

As I mentioned, we all have blind spots. They often occur because we judge ourselves based on our intentions while others judge us based on our actions. We may intend to provide our customers with a high-value solution to their problem, but when the customers don't see it that way, we may think something is wrong with them. The real problem, however, is that our actions haven't demonstrated the value to them in a way that is visible to them.

If we become aware of our blind spots, we can work around them. The first step is to take the assessment in this chapter. Seeking the counsel of a friend or mentor whom you trust and asking that person, "What am I missing?" is another way to get insight into your blind spots.

HAZARD #2: ACTIVITY TRAP

With all the data, information, and noise coming at us each day, it's easy to become consumed by it, but mindless activity prevents people from achieving their goals. On average, people tap into less than 50 percent of their potential. They end up going through the motions day after day and letting circumstances out of their control dictate their outcome. This leaves people feeling disempowered. The good news is 10 percent of life is what happens to you and 90 percent is what you do with it. By igniting your selling potential, you will feel empowered, regardless of your circumstances. The first person you have to sell is yourself. We sell or unsell ourselves every day by the choices we make.

> *The first person you have to sell is yourself. We sell or unsell ourselves every day by the choices we make.*

To avoid the activity trap, it's critical to know what to say no to. The most successful people—whether they're athletes, sales professionals, executives, or something else—say no more often than they say yes. Another way to avoid the activity trap is to be intentional about which actions you take. Know your customer, know yourself, gain clarity on your destination, create written goals and an action plan, and be intentional about what you do so you can have a positive influence on those you interact with.

HAZARD #3: WINGING IT AND CRUISE CONTROL

The hallmark of a great leader is preparation. While winging it is easy and requires no planning, it's a formula for failure. The formula for success includes a plan, a purpose, a process, and a price. If you are missing any of those, you will not only be leaving potential on the side of the road, but you will also be setting yourself up to fail.

When we do something every day, like driving and selling, it's easy to go into cruise control. When we go into cruise control, we risk lowering our bar, staying in our comfort zone, and experiencing blind spots.

Everyone can get to their desired destination, accelerate revenue, achieve results, and develop strong relationships with the right roadmap, practice, and navigation. That's what this book is all about.

HAZARD #4: ENTITLEMENT

Accept responsibility for your personal growth and productivity. The key is to avoid the hazard of thinking your company should be perfect. No company, culture, or leader is perfect. Igniting your potential starts with you. You are in the driver's seat. My aim is to empower you to take the wheel and get on the superhighway to accelerate revenue and achieve your desired results.

> *"The best way to predict your future is to create it"*
>
> **—ABRAHAM LINCOLN**

HAZARD #5: BEING THE EXPERT

When things are green, they are growing; when they are ripe, they rot. The number-one denominator of success is personal growth. Someone who develops the mindset of a beginner is inquisitive, cares, and focuses on delivering value to the customer. That will lead to more buy-in, selling more faster, and greater overall success.

HAZARD #6: LACK OF BELIEF IN SELF OR OTHERS

When people don't know their unique gifts and strengths, they reach a point where they feel something is missing. When people lack purpose, they feel empty and lack drive. The flame goes out, and they zigzag through their career and life wondering what they should do next. That doesn't have to happen.

If you lack belief in yourself, that lack of belief will translate to others and impact your relationships. The good news is that you can ignite your belief in yourself with Accelerator 3, which will build confidence. Confidence is needed to sell and succeed in life. As you build confidence, you will become more successful.

HAZARD #7: WRONG METRICS

Measuring the wrong activities, ones that don't lead to the end result, is one of the most common hazards individuals, teams, and organizations experience. For example, a contracts team measuring the number of requests for proposals and proposals submitted does not help drive sales. A better metric would be the win/loss ratio or the number of proposals won as compared to the total proposals submitted. I love metrics and believe in cutting through the clutter to identify the right ones that help individuals and organizations succeed. It's especially important to focus on increasing selling time and removing as many nonselling activities as possible from your plate.

As you continue through the rest of the book, keep these hazards in mind. Throughout this process, you will be looking to identify those pitfalls and behaviors that slow you down or take you off-road and replace them with those things that will help you accelerate on your road to success!

ACCELERATOR 1 ACTION ITEMS

CHECKLIST: STRATEGIES FOR ACCELERATION

☐ Take the assessment by going to: **www.IgniteYourSellingPotential.com** to find out how much of your selling potential you are currently using today. You can do so by clicking on the WHAT'S YOUR SCORE button on the website.

WHAT'S YOUR SCORE?
MY SELLING POTENTIAL

☐ Know your score and identify your opportunities for growth.

☐ START NOW so you can realize and ignite your selling potential.

☐ List your 30/60/90-day goals for applying what you learn as you read this book.

☐ Be aware of potential hazards so you can avoid them on your road to success!

ACTION STEP: WHICH HAZARDS HAVE YOU EXPERIENCED?

At the end of each chapter, you will have an opportunity to identify which activities are preventing you from reaching your goals. Then, all you have to do is release and replace them with what is outlined in each accelerator to achieve your goals.

There are three simple ways to release an activity:

1. **Discard it.** This means you simply write it down on a piece of paper and then tear it up and throw it in the trash.

2. **Delegate it.** These are activities that need to be done but can be done by someone else. Hand them over. Don't waste your valuable time doing things that don't accelerate revenue and achieve results.

3. **Defer it.** Prioritize and schedule when it needs to be done on your calendar. Don't feel everything has to be done right away.

Next, replace the activity with the action that is going to produce your desired results. The key is to replace it right away so you don't fall back into the activity trap of unproductive actions and your old habits.

Here is an example:

Transform Activity into Productivity® to Ignite Your Selling Potential and Drive Sales Fast.

Activity that prevents me from achieving my goal	Action that ignites my potential. Action that drives productivity to my goal
I have not defined what success looks like to exceed expectations for my role.	Define success professionally with approval from my manager to exceed expectations for my role within 30 days from today.

Why is this important? You could be wasting valuable time and resources spinning your wheels by not having clarity around what success looks like in your role. As a result, you could miss the chance to exceed your manager's expectations.

I remember listening to a speaker say, "The saying used to be, if we continue doing what we have always done, we will get what we have always gotten. This is not true anymore. With the rate at which the marketplace is moving and technology is advancing, if we continue doing what we have always done, we will get less." Perhaps you have been successful in the past without some of these accelerators. That simply means you have more potential to ignite, and by igniting it, you will sell more.

TRANSFORM ACTIVITY INTO PRODUCTIVITY®:
APPLY, RELEASE, AND TAKE ACTION

1. What did you learn that you can **apply**?

2. What activity is holding you back from achieving your goals that you can **release**?

3. When can you **take action** to achieve your desired results?

YOU'RE IN THE DRIVER'S SEAT
YOU CHOOSE!

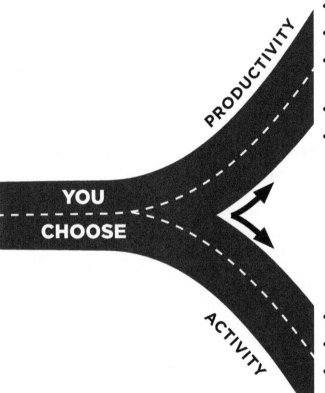

PRODUCTIVITY

- Repeatable Revenue
- Predictable Results
- Profitable and Sustainable Growth
- ↑ Job Satisfaction
- ↑ Personal Satisfaction

YOU CHOOSE

ACTIVITY

- Inconsistent Revenue
- Unpredictable Results
- Low Profit
- Unsustainable Growth
- ↓ Job Satisfaction
- ↓ Personal Satisfaction

KNOW YOUR CUSTOMER

IDEAL CUSTOMER + ALIGNMENT + STEPS
TO ACQUIRE = ACCELERATION

The purpose of business is to create and keep a customer.

—PETER F. DRUCKER

Successful people build relationships with their internal and external customers. Focusing on top-line revenue is not enough. Successful individuals, teams, and organizations focus on generating profitable revenue and creating differentiated value during every interaction. Knowing your ideal customer is essential to creating differentiated value and accelerating profitable revenue and results fast.

The reality is many people call on customers who are not ideal. Thus, they don't generate the profit or growth needed to achieve their desired goals and results. Competition is getting tougher and tougher in every industry, and not everyone is equipped to handle it. As a result, they get distracted with activity, lose focus, and don't get to their destination on time. The good news is that if you are experiencing any of these challenges, you can learn how to navigate around them and learn what it takes to succeed.

Knowing your ideal customer is the first step in establishing long-term relationships and growing your revenue profitably. Sales professionals, managers, and executives, as well as any department supporting sales, must evaluate whether they are targeting the ideal customer, if they truly understand their customer, and whether they are able to deliver differentiated value during every interaction.

By the end of this chapter, you will understand how to strategically identify who your ideal customers are, know the steps to acquire them, and gain a competitive advantage to generate profitable revenue fast. Strategically focusing on the most profitable customers is how you gain the most revenue.

SETTING YOURSELF APART

I recently worked with a sales team that was in a highly competitive market and trying to differentiate itself from its competitors. In the past, team members had grown their top-line revenue but didn't know how to grow their bottom-line revenue. We identified their ideal customer and their profitable customers and segments of their business. Next, we created focused goals and action plans to get more customers. Lastly, we trained the team to create a compelling and differentiated value proposition so price was not an issue.

In a very short time, the entire team was refocused on which customers they needed to call on and how to create value to raise profitability. This also optimized the customer experience because they were able to articulate differentiated value. Within

12 months, they increased profitability 20+ percent. Sales professionals and their teams can sell if they have clarity and focus on the ideal customer and align their internal resources to deliver differentiated value to their customers. That is how they can effectively set themselves apart from the competition.

Organizations can also set themselves apart from the competition when it comes to their internal customers. The most successful organizations know their people are their greatest asset. Southwest Airlines has demonstrated outstanding performance and continues to differentiate itself in the marketplace. The airline now has a TV commercial stating, "The Southwest difference is that people are at the heart of everything we do." I had an opportunity to talk with an executive from Southwest Airlines, and I was impressed with the investment Southwest makes in its internal customers, its people.

Successful leaders recognize the importance of working with and through others to achieve results. Successful people at any level know their internal and external customers and develop collaborative relationships with them. They assess and seek to understand the needs, priorities, and goals of their cross-functional partners, supervisors, and direct reports. They create win-win solutions for the customer and company to optimize the customer experience. I call this working horizontally as well as vertically.

Conversely, unsuccessful people who lack buy-in and followership often neglect the needs of internal and external customers. They don't prepare, plan, and focus to consistently deliver differentiated value during each interaction.

One of the first questions I ask when I am considering partnering with a company or making a major purchase is, "Who is your ideal client or customer?" Why? Because if I'm not an ideal client, it will not lead to a productive conversation or long-term relationship. If I'm not an ideal client, the company will not be able to satisfy my short- and long-term needs. Thus, I need to go elsewhere. On the flip side, if I find a vendor or partner to whom I am an ideal client with similar values, I know the likelihood of developing a mutually beneficial, long-term, profitable relationship for both parties is greater.

I have seen firsthand how much more people and teams can sell if they have clarity and focus on the ideal customer and align their internal resources to deliver value to that customer. Whether you are a new hire, manager, or executive, all of you can benefit from knowing your ideal customer and becoming a customer advocate.

CALL TO ACTION FOR NEW HIRES

New hires who don't have clarity about the ideal customer will be less successful. As a new hire, use this book as a roadmap to sales acceleration during your first 90 days to get the greatest impact.

SEVEN SIMPLE STEPS TO KNOW YOUR CUSTOMER

These steps have helped thousands of sales professionals, managers, and executives during the past seven years. Be sure to take time to understand the ideal customer and work together within and across your department to have a visual picture of the ideal customer you are targeting to generate profitable revenue fast. This is an excellent discipline to revisit quarterly as you assess your revenue and profitability and plan for the next quarter.

1. IDENTIFY AND PROFILE YOUR CUSTOMERS

By identifying and creating a profile of your internal and external customers, you will find new ways to collaborate with them and accomplish their priorities (and hit your goals). Keep in mind that many people think their customers are only external. They don't think of internal colleagues and strategic partners or even employees as customers. As you identify both types of customers, focus on adding value to *everyone* with whom you interact. In other words, serve those around you. The most successful leaders and organizations view their people as their greatest asset. Your approach to creating a profile can vary depending upon the strategy, structure, size, and resources of your organization. For example, you can do a profile as a department or take a more holistic approach of combining the marketing, sales, and education teams together to create one focused profile.

Each profile should identify your internal and external customers and how you can collaborate with them to develop win/win relationships. Use the questions in this chapter to develop your profiles, and, again, keep in mind *all* the people with whom you interact. I believe in servant leadership and servant sales. That means adding value to everyone you interact with: customers, colleagues, employees, and partners. To achieve a 360° customer experience, list your customers in each of the circles in the diagram.

360° CUSTOMER EXPERIENCE

To achieve a 360° customer experience, list your customers in each of the circles below.

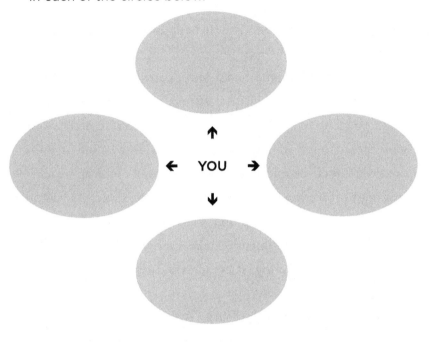

QUESTIONS TO ASK YOURSELF:

- Who are your internal and external customers?
- How can you collaborate with each customer to develop win-win relationships?
- What are each customer's needs or challenges, goals, and priorities?
- How can you optimize their experience and help them succeed?
- What can you do to develop a long-term mutually beneficial relationship?

- How can you deliver value during each interaction to help them overcome their challenges and achieve their goals and priorities?

QUESTIONS TO ASK YOUR CUSTOMER:

- If they are currently buying from you, you may ask them, "What do you like most about doing business with our company, department, or team?"
- What is of greatest value to you when working together?
- On a scale of 1–10, 1 being low and 10 being high, how would you rate your customer experience with our company, department, and/or team?

2. IDENTIFY YOUR BUSINESS OBJECTIVE TO EXECUTE YOUR SALES AND BUSINESS STRATEGY

The customers you target need to be in line with your business strategy. For example, if your objective is to grow revenue profitably, your two key success factors are high revenue and high profit.

Quadrant 2: High Revenue, Low Profit	**Quadrant 1:** Ideal Customer. High Revenue, High Profit $500 K in annual purchases. Average Deal size < $150+K. Located within a 500 mile radius of the headquarters
Quadrant 3: Low Revenue, Low Profit	**Quadrant 4:** Low Revenue, High Profit

REVENUE

PROFIT ⟶

3. SEGMENT CUSTOMERS INTO A, B, AND C GROUPS TO ACCELERATE PROFITABILITY

What is the fastest path to revenue and profitability? Is it growing existing customers, partners, or channels or gaining new customers, partners, or channels? Don't wait for marketing or another department to do this. Regardless of your role, take responsibility for understanding who your ideal customer is.

4. IGNITE, ALIGN, AND PLAN—TURN WONDERING INTO WINNING!

It's critical for every department impacting sales to have alignment and laser focus on the customer. This is where so many organizations, teams, and individuals miss out on growing revenue and achieving profitability and results. Make sure you incorporate your identification, communication, targeting, and business development initiatives within your sales and marketing team planning. Taking an integrated approach with marketing and sales is a better use of talent and resources. Aligning these functions and departments to enable and support sales makes it easier for your sales team to succeed in executing your brand, create a consistent client experience, and accelerate sales. Secondly, fueling strong relationships turns developing customers into long-term clients and enthusiastic advocates.

ALIGNMENT + IDEAL CUSTOMER + FOCUS ON DELIVERING VALUE = HIGH REVENUE + HIGH PROFIT + CONSISTENT BRAND
= POWERFUL CONSISTENT CLIENT EXPERIENCE

5. MAP THE STEPS TO ACQUIRE A NEW CUSTOMER/CLIENT

It is really important to visually map out the steps to acquire a new client. I call this the buying cycle. If you don't take time to prepare and plan, it makes it harder for your client, or customer, to do business with you. Even if you are not in a formal sales role, it's important to map this out and follow a process to make it easy for any internal/external customer to do business with you.

6. SOCIALIZE THIS

Educate your entire team, department, and other departments. Make sure everyone in your organization knows who your ideal customer is. Discuss how you can work together to deliver value to these customers.

7. FOCUS ON ACQUIRING, SERVING, AND RETAINING MORE OF THESE IDEAL CUSTOMERS

This is key. Stay in your sweet spot and focus everyone on the ideal client.

Without these simple steps, sales will not have the support of marketing and a common understanding of the ideal customer, and marketing will develop materials and resources focused on the less-than-ideal customers.

HAZARDS TO AVOID

The seven simple steps to know your customer are designed to avoid costly hazards. What is the cost of not knowing your ideal customer? Wasting valuable time and resources on the wrong customers. Low-profit and low-revenue customers can consume as much if not more resources than your ideal customers. Many of my clients say that 80 percent of their teams are focused on low-profit customers. Some teams don't know who their ideal customer is. Thus, they end up exhausting valuable resources on low-profit customers. High-performing teams avoid this by gaining a laser focus on the ideal customer.

Another hazard you can avoid by knowing and focusing on your internal customer is that of losing touch with your people. Tom Peters and Nancy Austin, authors of *A Passion for Excellence,* say, "The number one managerial productivity problem in America is, quite simply, managers who are out of touch with their people and out of touch with their customers." John Maxwell says, "I think one possible explanation is that some managers don't value people."

My experience is that when managers don't value people, customers don't value the company. **It's impossible for customers to feel valued when employees are not valued.** Value yourself, value others, value your team, and value your company. I believe the same applies to people selling. Successful people and high-performing teams who gain buy-in value their customers, team, and company. They generate revenue and achieve results by developing relationships and valuing their customers.

ACCELERATOR 2 ACTION ITEMS

CHECKLIST: STRATEGIES FOR ACCELERATION

- ☐ Identify and profile your customers.
- ☐ Segment to accelerate.
- ☐ Ignite, align, and plan.
- ☐ Map the buying cycle.
- ☐ Socialize this—educate everyone on who your ideal customer is.

PRODUCTIVITY TOOLS

- ■ Segment to Accelerate
- ■ Buying Cycle

To gain access to powerful productivity tools, online learning and courses for acceleration, go to:

www.IgniteYourSellingPotential.com

Ideal Customer + Alignment + Steps to Acquire = Acceleration

TRANSFORM ACTIVITY INTO PRODUCTIVITY®:
APPLY, RELEASE, AND TAKE ACTION

1. What did you learn that you can **apply?**

2. What activity is holding you back from achieving your goals that you can **release?**

3. When can you **take action** to achieve your desired results?

GAIN CLARITY ABOUT YOURSELF, YOUR ROLE, AND YOUR DESTINATION

CLARITY OF SELF + ROLES + DESTINATION =
ACCELERATION TO YOUR DESTINATION

The Self exists as a potential to be realized. The essence of knowledge is self-knowledge.

—PLATO

Most people spend more time planning their vacations than thinking about their personal and professional goals or what I call their destination. Vacations are great, but to be successful, you have to gain clarity about who you are, where you want to be, and what others expect of you. Knowing yourself and what is expected of you will help you build upon your strengths and better define your destination. Knowing what drives you will help you gain leverage to achieve meaningful results along the way.

As you gain clarity, you can make intentional, strategic choices that will help you arrive at your desired destination and achieve your desired results. People who have clarity can avoid costly hazards and are more prepared to handle the unexpected.

> *To ignore the unexpected (even if it were possible) would be to live without opportunity, spontaneity, and the rich moments of which "life" is made.*
>
> —STEPHEN COVEY

By the end of this chapter, you will have gained clarity about yourself, your roles, and your destination, which will ignite your potential and transform activity into productivity®.

FINDING YOUR WAY

All too often, people get stuck or fail to achieve their goals due to one or more of the following reasons:

1. They are not clear on the outcomes they want to achieve or what is expected of them, because they lack clarity on their role and destination.

2. They do not know themselves well enough to know how to change their behavior to gain leverage and achieve results.

3. They are too consumed with activity and working *in* the business, instead of stepping out to work *on* the business.

Gaining clarity about your role and destination will help you navigate around challenges to get to your desired destination. Before I became a sales manager, I got clear on the fact that I wanted my team to be number one, and I was going to work hard to achieve that. Then, I sought advice from the top four most successful sales managers in our company, which sold innovative medical products and services. They each had specific things they did to build winning teams.

- Patsy created a vision that was focused on being number one and making a difference in the lives of patients.

- Janet did a great job of focusing her team on the top three things they needed to do to differentiate their product from the competition. She walked me through what she expected from her sales reps during every field visit.

- Keith told me how he successfully built a cohesive team and leveraged his resources.

- Vince shared with me how he set very clear guidelines and expectations.

When I reached out to these people, I asked them a series of questions. I took notes on what I learned and then worked hard to develop a 90-day success roadmap to get off to a fast start. Knowing that what I was applying had already worked for others gave me confidence. Much of my success stems from learning what others have done to succeed, making it my own, applying it, and then, refining it.

If you want to avoid a slow start and achieve fast results, consider seeking out best practices. Why reinvent the wheel? The good news is that you don't have to know everything. You simply need to reach out to those who know what you don't and ask for help. The key is to practice this proactively. If you wait until you need a new plan, it may be too late. As John Wooden says, "The time to prepare is before you need it."

How do you get to your destination? Zig Zigler says, "When you sow an action, you reap a habit; when you sow a habit, you reap a character; and when you sow a character, you reap a destiny." Bruce Norman says, "You can't feel your way into a new way of acting, but you can act your way into a new feeling." **Act out your destination!**

HAZARDS TO AVOID

Avoid the hazards of falling into the activity trap, letting uncontrollable circumstances dictate your success, and going through the motions and running the risk of arriving at a less than desirable destination. Be proactive and take the wheel. You are in the driver's seat!

ROAD TO REVENUE AND RESULTS

Success is what you envision and aspire to become. Imagine there are no limits. What does success look like to you?

> *What does success look like to you?*

I enjoy helping emerging leaders gain clarity on their career goals and chart out their career development plan. One of the things people often struggle with is the lack of a clear path or road to success. As they plan their goals, I always encourage them to define success professionally *and* personally. An integrated, holistic approach is most successful. When they are not clear on what success looks like both personally and professionally, it's really tough to make good decisions. Once they follow these steps, they gain a lot of clarity on what they are gifted at, want to do, and how best to make decisions.

The same goes for even the most seasoned executive. You have to ask yourself, "Am I working toward my dreams? Am I leveraging my gifts and strengths every day to get to my destination?"

> *You have to ask yourself, "Am I working toward my dreams? Am I leveraging my gifts and strengths every day to get to my destination?"*

There is a big difference between a spark and a flame. Everyone has a spark—a dream, passion, and potential waiting to be discovered and ignited. You do also! The question is, have you found it? If you have found it, have you developed it? Are you working toward your dreams and leveraging your gifts and strengths to get to your destination? It's only when you find your spark and ignite it that you can realize and maximize your potential.

A client once introduced me to a colleague whom he thought could benefit from my services. As I met with this manager and got to know him, I could see his giftedness and potential. I asked him several questions, and he became very enthusiastic as he shared with me that he wanted to advance his career. But he didn't know what he wanted to do next. It was evident he didn't know himself well enough to

> *Whatever you do, don't stamp out your spark! Instead, ignite it!*

chart out a career development plan. So we agreed to meet two weeks later to discuss how I could help him get there.

As we sat down a second time, he told me that after our initial meeting, for the first time in a number of years, he had a spark again. He was inspired and motivated to think about how he could contribute in a bigger role within his organization. He had previously wanted to leave his position because he didn't feel he could grow. He shared with me that he met with his vice president to map out some development opportunities but was really struggling with what he wanted to do next. We agreed that knowing what career path to take was challenging for him because he didn't have clarity on his gifts and strengths or on what success looked like to him. We reviewed a process to help him take that spark and turn it into a flame. That process is here, in the chapter, for you to apply. All you have to do is walk through the questions and exercises. In a short time, you can ignite your potential and gain clarity on what success looks like to simplify your decision making and ensure your will be successful for years to come.

How about you? How about your team? Do you *and* your team have a spark or a flame? What are you doing to gain clarity about your dreams? Many people don't know how to kindle that spark. It's important for me, as a leader, to help my employees and team ignite their potential and maximize it so they can build upon their gifts and strengths and feel valued. If you are an executive and have not experienced the value of having a team of ignited individuals who are maximizing their

> *"The most successful organizations and executives recognize that their people are their greatest asset."*

potential to achieve results, you may be asking, "What value does this have to my business outcomes?"

The managers who tap into the potential of their team increase engagement and productivity and achieve results faster than those who don't. Note: It starts with potential, not productivity. Doing so helps people add value to their customers, exude passion and confidence, and meet or exceed expectations and results. When I scaled a business from $5M to $139M in revenue in less than three years, I did it by igniting and maximizing the potential of the individuals and team.

> *Note: It starts with potential, not productivity.*

It's okay to be a little unclear about your destination. By completing the questions and action items in the Strategic Development Plan that follows, you'll gain clarity. Go to the courses with online learning to gain access to additional powerful tools that will assist you in gaining clarity.

CREATE YOUR STRATEGIC DEVELOPMENT PLAN

To get started, take out a piece a paper and answer the following questions. You may not have answers right away, but the more you work at it, the more clarity you will get.

1. DEFINE SUCCESS IN YOUR ROLE PROFESSIONALLY

Ask yourself, "What is required for success in my role to meet and exceed expectations?"

I never strive to meet expectations; I strive to exceed them. Your company hired you to perform. Opportunities for advancement, additional responsibility, and rewards come to those people who exceed expectations. My team always knew that I had high expectations for each individual on the team to exceed our goals. They all knew we were playing to win. To build a winning team, I expected them to complete one another, not compete with one another. I expected each person to succeed in delivering differentiated value to our customers and helping our customers succeed.

> *Raise your bar! Always strive for excellence and to exceed expectations.*

Raise your bar! Always strive for excellence and to exceed expectations. **Ask your manager, "What are your goals and expectations for me? What does exceeding expectations in my role look like?"** If your manager doesn't have an answer, develop your own expectations for excellence. My expectations of myself in my role were always higher than my employer's.

Regardless of your role—which may be in sales, as a manager, or in some other role that impacts sales—it's important to gain role clarity. You can't underestimate its importance. In my experience working with sales teams and executives, when people are not performing, when they are not meeting and exceeding expectations, one of the problems is, typically, that they don't have role clarity. The manager has one expectation, employees have another, peers and direct reports have yet another. Lack of role clarity becomes a catalyst for low performance. Clear expectations are critical for productivity and performance.

LACK OF ROLE CLARITY = LOW PERFORMANCE

Without role clarity, everyone has different expectations. Different expectations lead to low performance. Fill out the following to gain role clarity and alignment from all perspectives:

Managers' expectations for the role	Employees' expectations for the role
Peer expectations for the role	Direct report or customers' expectations for the role

It's important to keep in mind that you don't just do this once and then you're done. High-growth companies are continually changing, so expect change and take responsibility for knowing what is expected of you in your role at any given time. Keep in mind that as your manager and your organization changes, the expectations of your role may also change.

2. DEFINE SUCCESS FOR YOUR PERSONAL ROLES AND ASSETS

Ask yourself, "What is expected of me as a daughter and a sister? As a mother and wife or as a husband, son, brother, and father?

[Define the roles that apply to you.] What does success look like in each of those roles?"

I learned years ago when I attended a Stephen Covey time management seminar that it was important for me to look at all my roles and then set goals. Each week, I would list my roles and set goals for the week. That meant my professional as well as my personal roles.

Success to me is about strengthening my relationship with the people I love most. It was after this exercise that I began calling my younger sister and my dad every week. It was one of the best decisions I ever made. I am so grateful and happy that I made my dad a priority with those weekly conversations, especially now that he has Parkinson's disease and can no longer talk. I bring that happiness and grateful heart into the workplace, where I reflect on the positive things I learned from my dad.

I define "assets" as the valuable areas of your life, including things such as family, faith, career, community, and finances. I encourage you to be intentional and strategic about investing in each of these areas. When you do, these assets become more valuable and provide balance with work/life. When you define success and invest in all seven of these areas, they create a work/life balance. I call this having a balanced portfolio. When you gain clarity, you can make strategic intentional choices personally and professionally. You become more

> *When you gain clarity, you can make strategic intentional choices personally and professionally. You become more engaged in life, and that translates into higher engagement in the workplace.*

engaged in life, and that translates into higher engagement in the workplace.

CREATING YOUR BALANCED PORTFOLIO WHEEL

This section will help you define success as a whole person, both professionally and personally. This is something I am especially passionate about. When you are trying to make decisions on next steps in your career, trying to get a promotion or a new job or make good business decisions and lack a big-picture view, review and answer the questions in this chapter. When you don't have clarity, you are likely to zigzag and end up in a place, position, or company that is not a good match. This lack of clarity makes it really hard to make good business decisions and personal decisions, and the results can be devastating. However, once you have clarity, it makes it much easier to make decisions that are in the best interest of your employer, family, and yourself. You will be more satisfied with work and ready to contribute. This shows up in your interactions with internal and external customers.

One key to acceleration and sustainability is fueling a balanced portfolio wheel for your personal and professional life. Following is a framework that will provide visibility on what is important to you and what your level of satisfaction is in the top seven areas of your personal and professional life. It will help you see the big picture and make intentional, strategic choices to get to your destination. Successful people and organizations know the key to acceleration and sustainability is a balanced portfolio wheel. When you gain clarity by defining in writing what success means to you both personally and professionally, you will recognize the difference it makes. It will help you make intentional strategic choices in your current role and career along with your personal life. Do this now! Don't wait!

Guidelines: When you fill in what success looks like in each area one, three, and five years from now, be sure to use the first person. For example, for "Community," I wrote, "I enjoy giving back to the community and donate 10–15 percent of my time to purposeful charitable organizations. I make this a priority and find it gratifying to give."

Another thing to keep in mind is to not limit yourself. This is your picture of success, your dream, and there are no limits with dreams. Defining success is really defining your dreams and destination. If you can see it, you can achieve it. If you believe it, you can become it.

This activity provides clarity in planning, decision making, communication, alignment, and execution. It provides a balanced, holistic perspective for identifying your drivers of success, both personally and professionally.

TOP 7 ASSETS ASSET	WHAT DOES SUCCESS LOOK LIKE AND SOUND LIKE IN EACH OF THESE AREAS OF YOUR LIFE?	WHAT DOES SUCCESS LOOK LIKE AND SOUND LIKE IN EACH OF THESE AREAS OF YOUR LIFE?	WHAT DOES SUCCESS LOOK LIKE AND SOUND LIKE IN EACH OF THESE AREAS OF YOUR LIFE?
	One year from today	Three years from today	Five years from today (I like to use ten years. However, you may prefer five.)
1. Faith			
2. Family and Friends			
3. Fitness			
4. Financial			
5. Career			
6. Community			
7. Learning			

A balanced portfolio wheel allows you to make good decisions and leverage your time and talents to succeed both personally and pro-fessionally. I share this with you so you can make strategic and intentional choices, both personally and professionally. Why? Because I care about you!

> *A balanced portfolio wheel allows you to make good decisions and leverage your time and talents to succeed both personally and professionally.*

WHAT DRIVES YOU?

I believe we bring our whole selves to the workplace. Gaining clarity on both your personal and professional selves helps you ignite your potential in all areas of life. As you learn what drives you and what your destination is, you will ignite more potential than ever before. I see it every day with the clients I work with. I share this with you to encourage you to do the hard work required to realize the benefits.

Some people go through life never defining success or creating a balanced portfolio wheel. Most of the time, they wind up at a destination they are not satisfied with. They are counting down how many years they have until retirement. They dread their work. They say things such as, "Only nine years to go." I ask why, and they tell me they don't like their job or their leader is not a good leader. What it really boils down to is that they are disengaged with work and life. They show up physically but not emotion-ally. Disengaged people stay in the workplace, and they are takers instead of contributors. They ask, "What is the company going to do for me? How much can I take from this company?"

Engaged, successful people ask different questions. They show up ready to perform, to make a contribution, to get things done, to give to their team and employer. John F. Kennedy did a great job calling everyone in the country to a higher level of engagement when he asked, "Ask not what your country can do for you, ask what you can do for your country." The good news is that you can become engaged by asking questions and striving to contribute.

What is engagement, and why does it matter? When you get engaged, you will experience greater personal and professional satisfaction—not to mention success. The more you apply and practice what you learn in each Accelerator, the more confident you will become. You will ignite your potential and sell more when you are engaged.

WORK/LIFE ENGAGEMENT =
MAXIMUM SATISFACTION + MAXIMUM
CONTRIBUTION AND IMPACT

3. CREATE A COMPELLING VISION

Vision is what you aspire to become. It provides a picture of what you want to do with your career and life. It reflects your values, goals, and what you are excited about becoming.

To create your own vision, ask yourself,

- What do I love to do?

- What do I want to do?

- What positive feedback have I received from others in the workplace and personally?

- What lifestyle do I want to have?

- What is important to me and why?

- What do I stand for?

- What do I aspire to become?

These are all important questions to answer because you need to know what type of environment you want to be in as you build your personal and career vision.

All successful executives, teams, and individuals learn to work hard and play hard. The most successful ones know when to say no. Balance is essential. This balanced approach has helped me invest my time in the people I care most about and in initiatives that make a difference in the lives of others, which, in turn, makes a difference in my life. When all is said and done, I want my life to reflect making a difference and adding value to the lives of others. How about you? How do you want to invest your time and talent to make a difference?

Here are some examples of personal visions:

- To make a positive difference in the lives of my family, community, and all those I interact with.

- To become a leading expert and thought leader in my industry.

Here is an example of a career vision:

I will become a leader in my organization, helping transform it into an organization that values people as their greatest asset while, at the same time, being the best husband and father I can be.

THE POWER OF PURPOSE

Purpose is the *why*! Purpose ignites potential. Purpose is about gaining clarity on what your company stands for and what you stand for and want to accomplish.

People need to know why the organization exists. They need to know how their product or service delivers value and helps their customers. This clarity of purpose helps people make decisions and create actions that are consistent with the company purpose and vision. By the same token, having clarity on your personal purpose will help you make intentional strategic choices about how you spend your time. This enables you to live a life of meaning and to experience gratification by doing so.

Purpose is powerful! Purpose provides significance. John Maxwell talks about moving from success to significance. Someone can be successful as an individual performer, but to move to significance means you become purposeful and intentional about adding value to others. Purpose is a significant motivator. You will be able to ignite more of your potential when you gain clarity on your purpose.

> *Purpose is powerful! Purpose provides significance. Purpose is a significant motivator.*

Successful CEOs also recognize that defining purpose for the people in their organization ignites potential. One of my favorite vision statements is from Under Armour: "Empower athletes everywhere." That one statement ignites potential and provides purpose for each and every employee in their company worldwide.

The minute I walk through the doors of an organization, I can tell if it has a compelling purpose and vision. The ones that do are full of energy and focus on adding value to the lives of their customers. The companies that don't have people in their seats waiting to get out of the office. Furthermore, they don't even realize it. I want to encourage you to stay the course. If you do and are true to your purpose, you will ignite your potential. Potential will not and does not get fully realized or maximized without purpose. If you want to ignite your potential, get clear about your purpose and vision. Answer the questions in this chapter. If you don't know all the answers, that's okay. The more you ask, the clearer the answers will become. I learned my purpose when I was 14 years old and have refined it every year. It's crystal clear now, though it still takes effort.

4. DEFINE YOUR MISSION

Mission is how you will get there. Visualize success in your role and achievement of your vision.

Example of a vision statement: To become a leading expert and thought leader in my industry.

Example of a mission statement: Research where the industry is going and consistently provide innovative solutions and education to establish thought leadership.

Look at your mission and read it aloud weekly. Modify it as needed to fit to your aspirations, values, and goals. Vision and mission are essential to ignite your potential and make good decisions to navigate to your destination. They help you know what to say yes to and what to say no to.

5. WHAT ARE YOUR VALUES AND BELIEFS?

Beliefs are what you know to be true. An example could be some words of wisdom your mom or dad shared with you, such as

"You can do anything you set your mind to." That belief becomes something you know is true.

Values are what you deem important. Examples are integrity, respect, and customer focus. When someone values integrity or doing what they say they're going to do, they plan their day, week, and calendar around executing on their verbal commitments. If people don't have integrity, they don't intentionally put this value to work. In sales, that means they make commitments but don't follow through. This significantly impacts their revenue and relationships.

People often feel conflict when they take actions that are not in alignment with their values and beliefs. Sometimes, people's values and beliefs can be invisible to them, but values are a critical part of making good personal and business decisions. Personally, I don't know how people can make good decisions without identifying their values.

6. WHAT ARE YOUR GIFTS?

You were designed with special gifts. These are what you were designed for, what you are passionate about and yearn to use for the benefit of others. Using these gifts will give you great satisfaction and joy. It will give you fuel to fulfill your vision and sustain you.

Examples of gifts are teaching, leadership, wisdom, showing mercy, hospitality, and faith. If you would like to know your gifts, you can purchase spiritual gift assessments at amazon.com or other bookstores.

Many people go through life and never discover their gifts. As a result, they miss out on the fun of working and living in what author Scott Fay calls their sweet spot, not to mention achieving significance and success. When we combine our gifts with our strengths, which I'll talk about in the next section, we achieve near-perfect performance. Recognizing your gifts helps you understand what you are capable of. They are what you have been given to achieve a greater purpose. Gifts are to be given away. When you give gifts away, you help others succeed. You will find more passion and drive when you use and align your gifts and strengths with your purpose.

7. WHAT ARE YOUR STRENGTHS?

Strengths are different from gifts. The Gallup organization describes a strength as the ability to consistently provide near-perfect performance in a specific activity. The key to building a strength is to identify your dominant talents and then comple-ment them by acquiring knowledge and skills pertinent to the activity.

In the early '90s I read the book, *Now Discover Your Strengths* by Marcus Buckingham and Donald Clifton. From it, I learned that just because we have a strength doesn't mean we are strong in that area. However, if we develop our strengths, we will experience greater job satisfaction and near-perfect performance. In every encounter, I strive to figure out what people's gifts and strengths are so I can help them build upon them. People

You can discover your strengths by taking the strengths assessment found in the Gallup Organization's book, **StrengthsFinder 2.0** *by Tom Rath and online at Gallupstrengthscenter. com/Purchase/ en-US/Product.*

flourish when they discover, develop, and put their strengths to work.

You utilize more of your potential when you focus on developing, using, and building upon your strengths. You will experience more energy and motivation to achieve your goals, not to mention greater success personally and professionally. One of my strengths is strategy. I am very good at creating a fast path, a freeway that is proven to move the masses to accelerate revenue, achieve results, and get people to their destination. It's fun and rewarding to help individuals, teams, and organizations succeed, achieve their goals, and gain a competitive advantage.

8. ASK YOURSELF, "WHAT ARE THE TOP THREE THINGS I AM REALLY GOOD AT? WHAT ARE MY GREATEST ACCOMPLISHMENTS I AM MOST PROUD OF? WHAT ARE MY PREFERRED ROLES AND RESPONSIBILITIES?"

I know there are three to five things I am really good at. I could do them every day passionately and say no to everything else. Saying no helps us release those activities that don't produce results. For me, saying no helps me stay focused on using my gifts in the most impactful way to add value to the lives of others.

9. ASK YOURSELF, "WHAT CULTURES HAVE I THRIVED IN?" WHAT HAS BEEN YOUR FAVORITE POSITION YOU HAVE WORKED IN AND YOUR FAVORITE COMPANY YOU HAVE WORKED FOR? WHAT DID YOU LIKE

ABOUT WORKING IN THAT ROLE, ON THAT TEAM, OR FOR THAT ORGANIZATION?

If the culture matches what you look for and what drives you, you will be more satisfied, engaged, and contribute more.

Ask yourself, "What cultures have I thrived in?"

KNOW YOUR *WHY*

Daniel Pink, Simon Sinek, and others tell us that we are **more motivated and productive** when we understand why we are doing the work we do and the impact it has on others. Once you know why you do what you do and what drives you, you can organize and plan your work and life to align it with your why! This will improve your performance and your team's performance significantly.

Knowing what motivates you is essential to igniting your potential, increasing your productivity, and driving performance. If you don't know what motivates you, you will not be able to gain leverage on yourself to do what it takes to successfully generate revenue, achieve results, and increase your productivity.

Many people think sales professionals are just motivated by money. Salespeople often say money motivates them, but numerous studies state that money is not the main motivator. If money were the only motivator, why would people who have money be so driven? Successful people don't stop being motivated when they have money because money is not their primary motivator.

There are two types of motivators: intrinsic and extrinsic. If you rely only on extrinsic motivators, you will have a hard time motivating yourself. If you learn about what motivates you intrinsically, you will be able to motivate yourself when you don't feel motivated.

INTRINSIC: INTERNAL MOTIVATORS	EXTRINSIC: EXTERNAL OUTSIDE YOURSELF
Purpose and passion	Money
Job satisfaction	Achievement
Work life balance	Recognition
Personal satisfaction	Public recognition
Relationships	
Beliefs	
Values	

High-performance cultures know the importance of structuring a pay-for-performance, recognition and reward system to inspire and motivate employees to achieve goals. By contrast, underperforming teams don't pay attention to recognition programs or intrinsic motivators. Underperforming teams are typically led by underperforming leaders. These leaders don't understand motivation and say things such as, "I pay them a bonus if they achieve their goals, so why do I need a recognition program?" I have even heard some say, "I don't believe in motivating others." These same leaders want performance. What they don't understand is that motivation and performance are related.

This is especially important for sales teams. Sales professionals, like anyone else, are motivated by recognition and achievement. I remember winning award trips to Madrid and earning ring club and president's club awards and trips. I never cared about the award as much as the personal satisfaction of winning, while others wanted the money or public recognition. Some people are motivated more extrinsically and others intrinsically. What matters most is that you understand what motivates you, and, if you are a leader, to intimately understand what motivates your team. I learned this when I was a sales manager. I asked my team members for their input, and one of my sales reps recommended a sales rep of the month contest. So that's what we did. The winner had to show specific behaviors and performance, and the reward was a letter, a $200 gift certificate, and recognition in our region and the nation. My sales team loved it. I was pleasantly surprised at how something so simple and inexpensive inspired and motivated people. I feel that the best ideas come from my employees. When I managed sales teams and divisions, I worked hard at asking the right questions, listening to my team, and seeking their input. Together we consistently came up with a winning formula and accelerated our revenue to achieve results and deliver value to our clients.

Regardless of your role, by knowing what motivates you and keeping a laser focus on your destination, you can change how you work to drive results. For example, I am an extrovert and a people person. I would much rather be with people, speaking, teaching, and coaching than be in the office doing administrative work. At the same time, I know the importance of deadlines. If I focus on the benefit to the customer, I gain enough energy and motivation to do the less desirable aspects of my work. I also know that my peak concentration time is in the morning. So I prioritize my day to work on my most important priorities in the morning and reserve the afternoon for meetings with people because those meetings give me energy and play to my strengths.

Know yourself and your peak concentration times. Plan your toughest work, which requires the most energy, during your peak times of day. Plan the work that requires less concentration during your low-energy times of the day. Doing so helps you realize and maximize your potential.

CONSCIOUS VERSUS UNCONSCIOUS DRIVERS

The final thing you need to know about what drives you is the difference between your conscious and unconscious drivers.

Neuroscience tells us the mind has two components: the conscious mind and the unconscious mind. The reality is that the majority of our behavior comes from our unconscious self. Up to 90 percent of our behavior is driven by our unconscious mind.

This is why it's so important to outline your beliefs. As we strive to grow and venture outside our comfort zone, we can be held back by self-limiting beliefs. You see, our beliefs are what we know to be true. We cannot outperform our own self-image.

Top athletes and many peak performers recognize this and learn how to do what I call rescripting the self-limiting beliefs to achieve greater performance.

One model that describes this is the cognitive behavioral therapy model, also known as CBT. CBT basically focuses on the relationships between our thoughts, feelings, beliefs, and actions. It centers on the fact that we are each affected by our environment and belief system, which involves our current environment (family, friends, culture, job, workplace culture, successes, failures) as well as our past environment. Within each environment there is a cycle of five stages:

1. our cognitive thoughts and beliefs that drive

2. our emotions and feelings that drive

3. our relationships that drive

4. our behaviors and actions

5. our behaviors create consequences

I learned firsthand how this impacts performance when I started training for a marathon. I always told myself it was too hard or too much strain on my body. It wasn't until I struck up a conversation at a running group with a gentleman in his late 70s whom I didn't know that I changed the way I thought.

"So, do you run?" I asked.

"Yup."

"Have you ever run a marathon?"

"Yup."

"How many?"

"257. Seven in different countries."

Then the conversation changed. Burt asked me, "so you do run?"

I said "Yup."

"Have you ever run a marathon," he asked.

I said, "No."

He asked, "Why not?"

I said, "I don't think I can."

What do you think he said next? NOTHING. ABSO-LUTELY NOTHING. That conversation made me realize that my beliefs were holding me back from doing something I had not done before. I signed up for a marathon soon after that.

In order to break through that self-limiting belief, I followed the CBT model and began replacing the old negative beliefs with new ones that supported my vision and desired destination. It didn't happen all at once. It took work and perseverance, but

I accomplished my goal. I just had to remember that behavior is linked to beliefs. Our performance is a direct result of what we believe, think, feel, and do. The only person who limits my achievement is me. I am in charge of the outcome.

The gentlemen who inspired me to run my first marathon was Burt Carlson. He began running in his 50's, and at 83 he had run 300+ marathons. He is one of fewer than 200 people in the world who have run so many marathons.

Surrounding yourself with people who support your beliefs also helps. Changing your culture and company can help drive a different behavior. That's why the marathon success rate is so high for runners who join a marathon-training group. They are immediately surrounded by a positive culture that supports running a marathon and coaches who show you how to train.

Successful people adopt positive self-talk and positive thinking. Encourage yourself and think positive self-thoughts. Manage your thoughts, or they will manage you.

These relationships are depicted below in this restructuring framework.

COGNITIVE RESTRUCTURING FRAMEWORK

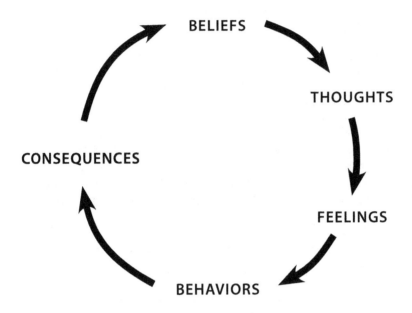

Empowerment means literally increasing your capacity to control your state of mind internally. The more you regulate your state of mind, the more powerful you will feel. The question is, who are you letting regulate your mind?

> *Empowerment means literally increasing your capacity to control your state of mind internally.*

You can change your outcome by using this process in reverse to change your thoughts, which in turn, changes your beliefs. If you want to be the number-one sales professional, then manage your thoughts to achieve that. If you are a manager and you want to build a winning team, manage your thoughts to win! Top performers, whether athletes or sales professionals, think differently to perform differently. Now that you know this, you can too!

Conversely, it's important to know what demotivates you. For me, it's a lack of purpose and value to others. I remember once being asked to do a sales coaching workshop for a team of sales directors. My client, who was in charge of development at a Fortune 500 company, was excited about hiring an author for day one and having me speak and teach on day two. He invited me to attend day one. The speaker started off by showing videos of himself being interviewed on CNN. He then had a lineup of several books he had written at the front of the room. As I listened to the speaker's opening, I thought, "I hope I can create as much value as this speaker." The next day it was my turn. I had been scheduled for just a half-day session, but at the end of my workshop, the sales directors rushed up to me and said, "I wish we had you for a full day and him for a half day!" I asked why and my client replied, "Because you gave us a lot more value than him. The previous speaker was more focused on himself than on us."

TAKE CHARGE OF YOUR OWN GROWTH!

It's not your employer's responsibility to ignite your potential. Igniting your personal potential is an inside job! Personal growth is the number-one factor that determines a person's success. *If your employer does not have an onboarding system built for speed to ignite your selling potential, take charge, and use this book as your own 30/60/90-day revenue acceleration plan.*

The only person you can change is yourself. If you want to be successful, develop a personal growth plan and use the action items that follow to create your own individual plan to succeed.

> *The one thing that separates winners from losers is winners take action!*
>
> —**ANTHONY ROBBINS**

You are in the driver's seat. You have the power to choose. What strategic and intentional choices can you make to discover and develop your gifts and strengths? Now that you have clarity of your vision, mission, and purpose, what growth steps can you take to arrive at your destination on time?

> *To gain traction, we need to take action.*

ACCELERATOR 3 ACTION ITEMS

CHECKLIST: STRATEGIES FOR ACCELERATION

- ☐ Build your strategic plan to *ignite your potential.*
- ☐ Define success professionally and personally.
- ☐ Gain clarity on what's expected of you in your role to meet and exceed expectations.
- ☐ Create a compelling vision and mission. Know your *why*, your purpose.
- ☐ Identify and leverage your gifts and strengths.
- ☐ Know what drives you and how to gain leverage on yourself.

PRODUCTIVITY TOOLS

- ■ Your Balanced Portfolio Wheel
- ■ What Drives You and Your Destination

To gain access to powerful productivity tools, online learning and courses for acceleration, go to:

www.IgniteYourSellingPotential.com

Clarity + Strategy + Intention + Choice

= Acceleration to Your Destination

"Faith in the endgame helps you live through the months or years of buildup."

—Jim Collins, *Good to Great*

TRANSFORM ACTIVITY INTO PRODUCTIVITY®:
APPLY, RELEASE, AND TAKE ACTION

1. What did you learn that you can **apply?**

2. What activity is holding you back from achieving your goals that you can **release?**

3. When can you **take action** to achieve your desired results?

PHASE II

PLAN

CREATE GOALS AND ACTION PLANS

FOCUSED GOALS AND ACTION PLANS +
CONSISTENT DAILY ACTION
= PREDICTABLE REPEATABLE RESULTS

Virtually nothing on earth can stop a person with a
positive attitude who has his goal clearly in sight.

—DENIS WAITLEY

People who have focused goals and action plans in writing accelerate revenue and achieve results with greater success than those who
don't. A recent Harvard study set out to discover why 3 percent of
Harvard MBAs made ten times more than the other 97 percent
combined. The study revealed the difference was that the top 3
percent had written goals and an action plan, had articulated their
goals out loud, and had established accountability for achievement of their goals.

The reality is that 97 percent of people don't have written goals and action plans, and thus, they leave their potential on the side of the road. The good news is that as you learn how easy it is to create written goals and action plans, you can ignite your potential to accelerate revenue and achieve your desired results.

I started formally setting goals when I was 15, but every year I learn something new. It seems the more I learn, the more I realize there is even more to learn. As I began setting goals and putting them in writing, I began to experience more and more success. I love the clarity that comes with writing goals and action plans. I also enjoy how striving for a goal helps me maximize my potential to become a better person by adding value to the lives of others.

The research, as well as my own experience, shows that successful people who consistently arrive at their destination on time have focused goals and action plans. Every sales team I have trained to create focused goals and action plans has achieved success. One sales team set a record by achieving the highest sales growth in 20 years. At a gathering to celebrate their success, one of the sales professionals said, "We would never have exceeded our sales goal if it wasn't for our focused goals and action planning process."

> *What are goals? Simply the dreams or desired results a person or team wants to achieve. What are action plans? Steps to achieve your dreams.*

In this chapter, you will learn a proven process for setting and achieving goals. Perhaps, you have set goals before and haven't achieved them. You are not alone. However, I want to encourage you to try this process because it works. If you use it, you will achieve your goals.

What are **goals**? Simply the dreams or desired results a person or team wants to achieve. What are **action plans**? Steps to achieve your dreams.

HAZARDS TO AVOID

I have to admit I failed to achieve some of my goals in the past. For example, when my friends were setting New Year's resolutions one year, I fell into the trap of setting my own, only to find out six months later that I didn't achieve them. Every January, in fact, my health club is packed with people who set New Year's resolutions. However, by the end of February, so many have failed that the crowd has already diminished. The hazard I have learned to avoid is setting resolutions, or any goals, with no process or plan in place to achieve them.

Another hazard to avoid is limiting your potential by not putting your goals on paper. **When individuals and teams have unwritten goals they will be less productive. The risk of spinning your wheels and going off-road is greater without the focus written goals provide. It leads to low motivation and low engagement when you keep your goals in your head.**

THE CASE FOR GOALS

- Did you know that the probability of completing a goal increases by 10 percent if you hear someone else state a goal out loud? Just by saying, "I want to write a book," or "I want to climb that mountain," you are more likely to do it.

- The same Harvard study found that having accountability appointments to check on your progress as you pursue your goals increases the probability of achieving your goal by 95 percent!

THE PROCESS

Goal setting and action planning are known as performance-enhancing strategies. A goal is simply an objective with a timeframe that you want to accomplish. While simple, it's also very powerful. You probably have some experience with goal setting by now and with achieving or not achieving your goals. The process I am going to share with you works every time. It is a combination of proven strategies that I have utilized successfully for 30 years to accelerate revenue, achieve results, and develop long-term, healthy relationships.

Regardless of how much you know about goal setting and how successful you have been in the past with setting, achieving, and exceeding goals, I believe that you will learn something new that you can apply from this process. **Here is the formula that works every time.**

1. TAKE TIME TO WRITE OUT YOUR GOALS

Some people set goals and fail and then never try again. I had someone tell me that they don't set revenue goals for their company because they never hit them. Hitting a goal has less to do with setting a goal and everything to do with developing an action plan and accountability to achieve the goals. So if you have set goals that you haven't achieved, I want to assure you

> *If you don't have time to write out your goals, you won't have time to achieve them.*

that you will succeed if you follow this process. If you don't have time to write out your goals, you won't have time to achieve them. It's that simple.

2. GAIN CLARITY

Goal setting is an iterative process. That means it may start off fuzzy before you move to clarity. I share that with you to encourage you. Clarity comes over time. If you don't have clarity when you start to set goals, be patient and keep working at it. The more you set goals, the clearer your goals will become. It's especially helpful if you have a skilled coach guiding you through a proven process of discovery.

In the workplace, it's very important to know what is expected of you in your role before you set goals, so you can meet and exceed expectations. In other words, people need to have role clarity before they can gain goal clarity. This is what we discussed in Accelerator 3. If your goals are not in alignment with what is expected of you, you are less likely to meet and exceed your performance expectations.

> *People need to have role clarity before they can gain goal clarity.*

4 ELEMENTS OF ROLE CLARITY

1. Boss' understanding (Role Description)	2. Employee's understanding of the role
3. Others' understanding (expectations from colleagues, cross-functional partners, direct reports)	4. Reality (how the role is demonstrated in actionable behaviors)

The same applies to what is required of you at home. If being a hockey coach for your son or tennis coach for your daughter is required of you, then you may choose not to take a role where you are traveling four nights a week. That is why in Accelerator 3 it's so important to define success both professionally and personally. I see a lot of people take on roles that conflict with their personal life and values. As a result, they go to work dreading their job and counting down the years until they get out of it. There is nothing wrong with their job; they just didn't plan and thus, they were not able to make strategic choices that were in alignment with their personal and professional goals.

3. SET SMART GOALS

As you begin to make a list of your top three to five personal and professional goals, I encourage you to use the **SMART goal setting process.** SMART stands for specific, measurable, attainable, relevant, and time-bound. In other words, if there is not a time in which the goal is to be completed, the question becomes "How will I know I have achieved it?" Vague goals without specifics, that aren't measurable and that don't have a timeframe attached don't help you get to your destination.

An example of a SMART goal might be: achieve $1M in incremental revenue growth by December 31, 2016, with a stretch goal of $1.2M.

4. NEXT ASK, "WHY DO I WANT TO ACHIEVE THIS?"

Goals without purpose or a *why* lack meaning and sustainability. Goals must be relevant to you to be motivating. Make them

relevant to achieving your vision and mission. Ensure they align with your values and definition of success, both personally and professionally.

One way to ignite your potential is to ask yourself, "Why is this goal important to me? How can I help more people succeed if I achieve this goal? What will I be able to do if I make more revenue and achieve my results?" One of the joys of generating revenue is being able to give more away. One of the joys of achieving results is helping someone else achieve similar results.

What I have learned is that when I describe why a goal is important to me, it helps me realize and maximize my potential at a higher level. When I have failed to achieve a goal, it's because I lacked a purpose, a plan, and a *why*. For example, one year, during a cold Minnesota winter when it was too icy to run outside, I put on five pounds. I was out with some friends on New Year's Eve and decided to share my goal of losing the weight I had put on. That was a joke because I didn't have a plan, metrics, or a *why*. Needless to say, I didn't achieve my goal until a couple of years later, after I learned I could be much more successful with a plan, the right metrics, and a *why*. I wanted to do more national speaking, which gave me a good *why* it was beneficial to drop five pounds: because I didn't want archived videos of myself carrying that extra weight!

5. IDENTIFY THE PAYOFF FOR ACHIEVING YOUR GOAL

Looking back at our SMART goal example above—to achieve $1M in incremental revenue growth by December 31, 2016, with a stretch goal of $1.2M—the payoff for achieving such a goal might be that you are able to pay for your child's college education

or take a vacation. This is important because you are more likely to achieve your goal if you can picture the payoff.

While I love to help my clients accelerate revenue and achieve results so they succeed personally and professionally, I am not motivated or driven by money alone. Revenue simply lets you help more people succeed. It's the currency for choices and options. Inspiring, equipping, and empowering more people to succeed personally and professionally is the payoff for me. Volunteering 10 percent of my time to nonprofit organizations that do purposeful work to add value to the lives of others, such as Feed My Starving Children, is motivating to me. I want to invest my time and talents where they get the greatest return in alignment with my purpose. What was fun about donating my service to FMSC this past year was that we were able to put together a strategic plan to generate enough revenue to feed 100 million more starving children around the world. Now that's an inspiring and motivating payoff.

6. BREAK YOUR GOALS INTO ACTIONABLE STEPS

Turn your goals into action plans. Without action plans they don't become reality. As you develop your action plan, ask, "What actions do I need to take quarterly, monthly, weekly, and daily to achieve this goal?" You will never change your sales results unless you change your daily actions. Our daily actions and habits are cumulative and turn into our weekly and monthly habits.

Nothing is too hard if you break it into bite-size pieces. When preparing myself mentally to run a marathon, I broke it down into five 6-mile runs, which adds up to 30 miles. A marathon is only 26.2 miles, but mentally, I planned for a stretch goal of 30 miles, which made 26.2 miles seem short! I ran the first four segments

at the same pace and then picked up the pace at the end to exceed my first goal and hit my stretch goal.

EXAMPLE OF HOW TO BREAK DOWN A GOAL

GOAL	$ SALES	$ SALES STRETCH GOAL	# OF DEALS STRETCH GOAL @ $110K EACH	WEEK 1	WEEK 2	WEEK 3	WEEK 4	+/- GOAL
Week	$20,833	$25K	.28					
Month	$83,333	$100K	1					
Quarter	$250K	$300K	3					
Annual	$1M	$1.2M	10					

- How many calls do you need to make?
- How many meetings do you need to have?
- How many demos do you need to do?
- How many proposals do you need to present by when to achieve your goal?
- What is the total of each of these activities you need to do weekly to achieve these goals?
- How will you reward yourself upon achievement? In other words, what is the payoff to you personally and to others?

If you are in another function, such as contracts and proposals, your goal may be to develop a proposal template that makes it easy for sales to differentiate themselves from the competition by the end of the quarter. Another goal may be to reduce your response time from seven days to two days and complete 400 proposals for sales per year, 100 a quarter, and 33–34 per month. Regardless of whether you have direct responsibility for sales or are in a function or department that supports sales, you can still create goals that enable sales to deliver differentiated value to their clients, accelerate revenue, and achieve results.

7. TRACK YOUR NUMBERS

How will you measure your progress toward your goal? Create a weekly scorecard with the numbers you need to reach daily, weekly, and monthly to achieve your goal and then track them regularly. This will help you see if you're on the right track. As I mentioned before, setting goals is an iterative process. It starts out blurry and then becomes clear. Breaking down your numbers and monitoring your quarterly, monthly, weekly, and daily goals provides a lot of clarity and makes the end goal more attainable.

You have to know your numbers even if they aren't revenue based! A sales team, for example, will almost surely have quarterly and monthly revenue targets, but a marketing team I worked with once set a goal of one press release and three new sales brochures per quarter. Those were their numbers.

Don't just do this in your professional role; establish numbers for the goals in all areas of your life. I like to use the balanced portfolio wheel approach that we discussed in Accelerator 3 by setting goals across the seven areas of my personal and professional life. That helps me keep the main thing the main thing and focus on what matters most personally and professionally. I find that I will not be satisfied if I focus only on work.

8. NEXT ASK, "WHAT RESOURCES ARE REQUIRED TO ACHIEVE MY GOAL?"

The most successful people maximize their resources. Resources may include an executive presence on a sales call or sales collateral such as a case study of other clients/customers who have benefited from your services. Many times, people don't feel they have resources until I ask them what their resources are.

For this step, you can do the following:

- Make a list of the resources you have access to in your role, department, and company.

- Rank those resources in order of how accessible they are and how helpful they are in achieving or exceeding your goal.

9. COMMIT TO THE ACTIONS YOU NEED TO TAKE

Decide the specific actions you need to take to achieve your goals and estimate the amount of effort those actions will take. Then, calendar your action items. This is really important. When someone says they're going to do something and don't follow through, how likely are you to do business with them? Managers who do this demotivate their teams. Sales professionals who do this lose sales. If you are going to achieve more, you need to plan to work harder to achieve your goals.

> *It's one thing to know what we need to do; it's another to do what we want to do. This takes discipline. The most successful people strive to develop daily disciplines.*

It's one thing to *know* what we need to do; it's another to *do* what we want to do. This takes discipline. The most successful people strive to develop daily disciplines.

One of the disciplines I work hard at each day is to calendar and schedule my action items. If I don't, they don't get done. I ask myself daily, what are my top three priorities for today and for tomorrow to achieve my goals?

10. REVIEW, REVISE, AND REFOCUS AS NEEDED

It's important to take time to reflect on your goals, to review what's working and what isn't, and then to revise to ensure success. I ask myself daily, "What did I learn, and what can I do better next time?" Every day, I learn new things and strive to improve. I ask myself those questions and then take time at the end of the day to reflect on the answers. It's one of my daily disciplines. In order to do it consistently, I schedule it on my calendar.

11. VISUALIZE AND EXPECT SUCCESS

A powerful way to keep your goals front and center is to create a vision board. I have done this for years. Simply take a large poster board and get some of your favorite magazines. Write your goals on the board in the first person. Cut and paste your favorite pictures on the vision board. Look at it regularly. I even like to have sales teams cut out their rewards for their goals and put them on their vision board. The very nature of visualizing your success and looking at your goals will help you achieve them.

12. DEVELOP A CADENCE CASCADE

You will need positive reinforcement as fuel to sustain you. I call this the cadence cascade. What is cadence? It's a sequence of performance activities that when repeated creates a rhythm of successful outcomes. If you miss steps in the sequence, it will affect the outcome. I like to make a list and then schedule time to do the things on that list in my calendar. This is all about setting up systems. A life

> *What is cadence? It's a sequence of performance activities that when repeated create a rhythm of successful outcomes.*

without systems requires a person to start from scratch every time they face a challenge or task. That takes way too much energy away from doing the activities that produce the greatest results.

What does a successful cadence look like? A cadence is a checklist of key activities to schedule on your calendar and with your accountability partner(s) and team, as applicable, which drives productivity, revenue, and results. Cascading the cadence means, simply, including the daily, weekly, monthly, quarterly, and annual commitments. This will help you stay disciplined as you drive to meet or exceed your goals.

You may be thinking, "There is no way I have time to plan." Perhaps you are not a planner by nature. I am a good planner, but I am a terrible filer, because I like to see all my files. To solve this problem, I hired a consultant to organize and systemize my filing system to make it easy for me. This helps me be productive and exceed my goals. You don't have to be able to do everything yourself. Decide what resources you need to accomplish your goals. Remember you are in the driver's seat.

13. CELEBRATE AND REWARD SUCCESS

Be sure to celebrate your progress monthly. If your culture does not have a reward system, establish your own. This is really important. Depending on your strengths and what drives you, you can build your own rewards for achievement of your goals. For example, someone who has a competitive strength likes to win and can be motivated by winning awards and contests. You can establish a reward system such as a trip for achieving your quarterly and annual goals. Someone else may choose to reward themselves by taking a week of vacation to volunteer or do a mission trip to serve others.

When I started my sales career, I worked for an emerging growth division of a company that had a lot of great contests, everything from award trips to Madrid and St. Lucia to ring clubs and president's club. I loved to win these contests. I learned that the contests helped me prioritize my time and energy to focus on the things that mattered to accelerate my sales. I didn't really care about the prize or the trip. I just liked the challenge of winning. It was a good motivator. I still set goals and rewards for my company today. What is equally important about achieving goals is the character you develop along the way. It's who you become as a result of stretching yourself and achieving new heights.

> *What is equally important about achieving goals is the character you develop along the way.*

STRETCHING BEYOND YOUR COMFORT ZONE

Now that you know the formula for setting and achieving goals, I want to leave you with these words of encouragement. One of my favorite quotes is from Thomas Edison. He said, "If we did all the things we're capable of doing, we would literally astound ourselves." I share that with you because people who achieve greater success set goals not based upon what they have accomplished but based upon what they want to accomplish. In other words, you don't have to look back at what you have done to set your goals going forward. If you set your goals by simply looking back, you will have impaired visibility. You will be unlikely to realize and maximize your potential. You may get a spark, but you won't get a flame. Sparks go out easily. Flames don't.

> *One of my favorite quotes is from Thomas Edison. He said, "If we did all the things we're capable of doing, we would literally astound ourselves."*

You simply need to look at what you want to accomplish. You see, you are capable of achieving whatever you want to achieve if you follow this proven process to achieve your goals. I once attended a meeting where I heard a speaker challenge us to grow our business tenfold. As I began to think about that, the first thing that came to mind was, "No way, that's not possible." That is limited thinking. Anytime you stretch yourself out of your comfort zone, it's easy to fall into the trap of doubt, panic, and fear, which becomes self-defeating. **The comfort zone is a beautiful place, but nothing grows there. Successful people learn to move from the comfort zone to the breakthrough zone.**

THE BREAKTHROUGH ZONE

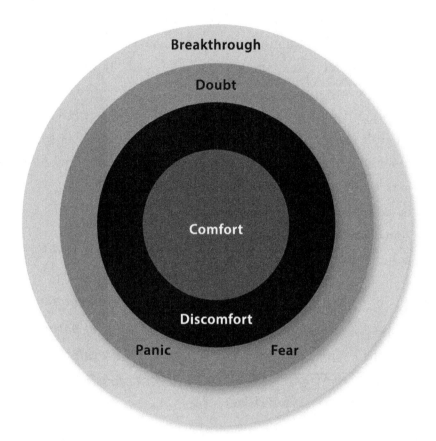

This happens all the time in sales. Once you achieve your sales goal, the next year the goal is raised. That's when I hear, "This is not attainable." The reality is that we are all capable of doing more than we think we are—at least ten times more! Believing that will help you focus on opportunities and look out at the horizon rather than in the rearview mirror. It's a way of thinking and envisioning success to achieve your goals personally and professionally. Every top athlete visualizes success and strives for performance at levels they have not achieved before. Then they put forth the effort and discipline by practicing relentlessly and focusing on the fundamentals to not just achieve their goals but also to raise the bar on their level of performance.

RAISE YOUR BAR!

I believe in order to maximize our potential, we need to set bigger goals that stretch us and help us achieve more than we expect of ourselves. If we set our bar too low, we limit our capability and potential to add value to the lives of others. There are many things that I never thought I could achieve until people expressed belief in me and challenged me to achieve greater heights. I also believe in the power of positive thinking and managing our thoughts.

MR. TRIUMPH VERSUS MR. DEFEAT

Why is it that we set our bar so low? In *Thinking Big*, author Dan J. Schwartz points out that your mind is a thought factory and the number-one factor in success is what you believe. He says we have two foremen in charge of our thought factory: Mr. Triumph and Mr. Defeat. Mr. Triumph is in charge of positive thoughts, why and how you can achieve your goals. Mr. Defeat is in charge of negative, self-defeating thoughts about why you can't achieve your goals.

Take this idea for a test drive by saying, "There is no way I can achieve my revenue or result target." Guess what happens? Mr. Defeat sends thoughts into your mind that support this belief. Mr. Defeat will tell you why it's not possible for you to achieve your sales goals.

Now tell yourself, "I can exceed my sales goal and my targets. My clients will buy a lot today." Mr. Triumph will find thoughts that support this belief. Mr. Triumph will tell you how you can achieve your goals and reinforce your belief.

If you focus more on Mr. Triumph, as Dan Schwartz says, you will produce more positive and productive thoughts. This takes up so much room in your thought factory that there won't be space for Mr. Defeat. In fact, you can even fire Mr. Defeat.

ACTION ITEM: SELECT A THOUGHT PARTNER

Imagine you have a BHAG, or a big hairy audacious goal, and are at the intersection of choice. Which thought partner will you choose? Mr. Defeat or Mr. Triumph?

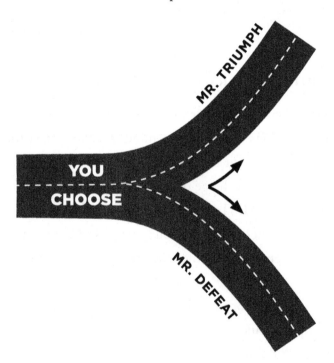

Here are the types of messages you can expect from each:

MR. DEFEAT	MR. TRIUMPH
You can't do that.	I have faith in you. You can do anything you set your mind to. You can.
This has never been done before. You have never done it before.	No breakthrough is achieved without raising the bar and setting new heights. Every goal is achievable.
That goal is unrealistic.	All you have to do is put one foot in front of the other and do the daily work required to get you to your destination.
This is crazy. Just stay the way you are. Don't set yourself up to fail.	This is possible. You will become more successful as you stretch yourself, and you will meet and exceed your sales goals. I always do!
I don't have the resources.	I will find the resources to exceed my goals.
My friends don't think it's possible.	I will make new friends who know it's possible.

I recently went to the Twin Cities Marathon to cheer on some friends. It was so much fun because the first person my husband and I ran into was my friend Burt, who had inspired me to run a marathon myself just a few years before. I had a chance to give Burt a big hug and tell him how he inspired me to think bigger than ever before. One day before Burt's 300+ marathon, I told him, "Good Luck!" He laughed and quickly replied, "I don't need luck. The race is won before we get there. We make our own luck!" I wholeheartedly agree.

You are in the driver's seat. You get to choose. So choose Mr. Triumph. Choose to fire Mr. Defeat! Say that with me. "Mr. Defeat, you're fired!"

Now that you've done that, ask yourself, "How high do I want to go?" How much of your potential do you want to leave by the side of the road?

> *You are better than your best.*
>
> —LIONEL L. NOWELL III

We all have more potential than we think. **I have faith in you that you can do far more than you have ever done before. Nobody starts out knowing how to do something they have never done before. Believe in yourself and others will too.** Ignite your potential by preparing, planning, and focusing on the fundamentals in each Accelerator, and you will be able to accelerate your revenue, achieve results, and fuel stronger relationships than ever before. You will be able to maximize your potential.

Successful people prepare, plan, and focus their time on the activities that drive productivity and help them to exceed their goals and arrive at their destination every time. Anyone can make their numbers and achieve their goals once. No one can consistently exceed expectations without preparation, planning, and focusing. Successful people continue to learn, improve, and create sustainable success. **Success is a habit achieved through consistently doing the things that drive results.**

ACCELERATOR 4 ACTION ITEMS

CHECKLIST: STRATEGIES FOR ACCELERATION

- ☐ Write down your goals. People who don't have a much higher rate of failure.

- ☐ Identify the payoff for achieving your goal.

- ☐ Break goals down into action items and quarterly and monthly targets. Know your numbers!

- ☐ Ask what resources are required to achieve your goal.

PRODUCTIVITY TOOLS

- ■ My 90-Day Action Plan

- ■ Goal Worksheets

To gain access to powerful productivity tools, online learning and courses for acceleration, go to:

www.IgniteYourSellingPotential.com

Clarity + Strategy + Intention + Choice
= Acceleration to Your Destination

TRANSFORM ACTIVITY INTO PRODUCTIVITY®:

APPLY, RELEASE, AND TAKE ACTION

1. What did you learn that you can **apply?**

2. What activity is holding you back from achieving your goals that you can **release?**

3. When can you **take action** to achieve your desired results?

PHASE III

FOCUS

MANAGE YOUR TERRITORY, TARGETS, TIME, AND PIPELINE

TIME + PIPELINE MANAGEMENT +
FOCUS = FASTER RESULTS

Spend 80 percent of your time with the
20 percent that produce the most.

—JIM ROHN

Whether you are in a sales role with responsibility for a territory, market, or vertical segment, or you are responsible for key projects within your department or organization, in order to be successful, you have to be able to effectively manage your time and pipeline to meet your targets and achieve your desired results. The reality is those who don't succeed or get passed up for promotions leave their potential on the side of the road because they lack the tools to prepare a plan or focus on areas that are key to success. The good news is that with a roadmap to results, everyone can ignite their selling potential and arrive at their destination faster.

By the end of this chapter, you will gain insight into how you can ignite your selling potential to manage your book of business; invest your time to gain a greater ROI; and manage your pipeline to accelerate revenue, achieve results, fuel strong relationships, and arrive at your destination on time.

I once worked with an organization that didn't have a pipeline when we got started or even know how to put one together, let alone manage it. We implemented a pipeline and key metrics along with several other key systems to drive results. Within one year, they gained an incremental $12M in revenue and built a $187M pipeline. Year two, they reached $25M in sales and year three, close to $50M in sales. I am always amazed at how fast individuals, teams, and organizations can accelerate revenue and achieve results when they implement these fundamentals that drive sales.

HAZARDS TO AVOID

Common hazards are falling into the activity trap and spending time instead of investing time to get a return. Other hazards are false confidence or what I call "Hopa Hopa Land." This happens when people lack a predictable pipeline that is qualified and as a result, lose credibility with management because they inaccurately forecast their numbers. The good news is that this can all be avoided.

SIMPLE STEPS TO MANAGE YOUR TERRITORY, TARGETS, TIME, AND PIPELINE

STEP 1: ASSESS YOUR BUSINESS

The first step to managing your territory, stakeholders, or book of business is to assess your business. You may be thinking this doesn't apply to you if you don't have a direct sales role with a specific territory, but it does. Your territory can be a geographical area, a market area, a vertical segment of accounts, or a key area of responsibility within your division or company. It's the area in which you are responsible for results.

SWOT ANALYSIS

We will start by doing a SWOT analysis. Simply fill in your strengths, weaknesses, opportunities, and threats.

SWOT stands for:

Strengths: internal characteristics of the business or team that give it an advantage over others in the industry.

Weaknessess: internal characteristics that place the firm at a disadvantage relative to others.

Opportunities: external chances to make greater sales or profits in the environment.

Threats: external elements in the environment that could cause trouble for the business.

Review the terms above and complete your personalized SWOT analysis by filling in the template provided.

	HELPFUL	HARMFUL
I N T E R N A L	Strengths:	Weaknesses:
E X T E R N A L	Opportunities:	Threats:

STEP 2: IDENTIFY YOUR TARGET ACCOUNTS OR KEY STAKEHOLDERS

The second step is to identify, within your area of responsibility, who your target accounts or key stakeholders are. For example, if you are with a marketing department, your key stakeholders could be sales, product management, compliance, training, etc.

STEP 3: SEGMENT YOUR MARKET AREA AND ACCOUNTS OR STAKEHOLDERS

This can be done using the targeting and ideal customer matrix you created in Accelerator 2. Segment your accounts or stakeholders according to the values that are most meaningful to you and your business so you can prioritize them. The A accounts are of greater value than the C accounts. This segmentation enables you to have laser focus on the accounts, stakeholders, and people who matter most to achieve your desired goals and results. Successful people know how to prioritize which accounts and stakeholders are most worth investing their time in. **After all, the enemy of best is good.** Next, use your segmentation to determine how often you need to communicate with your targets based upon your strategy and priorities.

STEP 4: QUALIFY PROSPECTS

You can qualify prospects against the ideal customer profile you created in Accelerator 2. This is your opportunity to make sure you aren't spinning your wheels by spending time on prospects, accounts, or stakeholders who are not ideal. You cannot be all things to all people. When individuals burn through valuable time and resources to meet with nonideal customers, it prevents them from achieving their goals. I am not saying don't call on C accounts or B accounts. Sometimes A accounts or stakeholders take longer to gain commitment. If they are competitive strongholds, they may have a longer sales cycle. It may take 12–18 months to convert them. In contrast, C accounts or stakeholders may be a smaller dollar amount and have a shorter sales cycle. Their time to conversion could be one to three months, which means they produce revenue faster. An A, B, or C account does not have to be classified on revenue and profit alone. It may also include strategic criteria such as being a key influencer.

STEP 5: KNOW YOUR NUMBERS
AND CREATE A SCORECARD

Identify how many accounts and what type of accounts you need to sell to in order to meet or exceed your goals and fill them in on the sample scorecard below. What products/services or solutions are you going to sell into each account to exceed your goals? Next, identify your top four to six zones (do not exceed six). Zones are the geographical areas in your area of responsibility or territory. List the cities, countries, or geographical area where you have the greatest upside potential to grow your revenue or market share. S 1–7 are the steps in the buying cycle. Enter the date at which that step is completed.

This is just one page of a scorecard. A complete scorecard, along with additional tools, is available in the online learning toolkit.

EXAMPLE OF TARGET ACCOUNT PIPELINE SCORECARD

TARGET ACCOUNT	CONTACT NAME	ZONE	A, B, C	EST. $	ECD	S1	S2	S3	S4	S5	S6	DATE CLOSED
1												
2												
3												
4												
5												
6												
7												
8												
9												
10												

Key: ECD: estimated close date; EST $: estimated $ in revenue you plan to close.

STEP 6: PROVIDE VISIBILITY AND TRANSPARENCY

Create your scorecard along with your manager and accountability partner. Review your pipeline weekly, on your own and with your accountability partner. Focus, focus, focus on advancing each account and stakeholder from step one to the next step to close.

STEP 7: PRIORITIZE AND PLAN YOUR TIME

> *Say no to activities that rob you of your time and attention and prevent you from reaching your goal. Say yes to activities that drive results and help you meet or exceed your goal.*

Say no to activities that rob you of your time and attention and prevent you from reaching your goal. Say yes to activities that drive results and help you meet or exceed your goal. The number-one indicator of productive people is how well they manage their time. Time management is a skill. That is why there are so many time management courses. I like to use the Pareto principle of 80 percent of your results are derived from 20 percent of your priorities. Or, applying it here, the top 20 percent of your priorities = 80 percent of your results.

THE NUMBER-ONE FACTOR IN PRODUCTIVITY: HOW YOU INVEST YOUR TIME

Good time management means investing time in the things that are most important to generate revenue, achieve results, fuel strong relationships, and get to your destination on time. **So what types of activities produce the greatest sales results?**

Presales activities:

- initial customer contact/cold calls
- lead identification/qualification
- creating sales plans
- creating call strategy/call plans
- competitor/industry research

Sales activities:

- sales calls/meetings/presentations
- informal relationship building/networking

Postsales activities:

- Continued relationship building
- Follow up, follow up, follow up

STEP 8: IDENTIFY THE RESOURCES YOU NEED TO ACHIEVE YOUR GOALS

The most successful people maximize their resources. It was always my top sales professionals and top performing employees who requested more resources. The squeaky wheel gets the grease. I never mind allocating more resources to these individuals because they use them wisely and achieve their targets.

STEP 9: WORK YOUR PLAN EVERY DAY

Each week reflect and measure your progress to your goal. Course correct as needed weekly, revising and refocusing as needed to achieve your goal. I like to build 15 minutes of reflection time into my daily agenda. I ask reflection questions tailored around my growth plan that help me learn and continually improve. Daily questions help me learn from experience and turn experience into insight and insight into daily improvement.

ACCELERATOR 5 ACTION ITEMS

CHECKLIST: STRATEGIES FOR ACCELERATION

- ☐ Complete a SWOT Analysis.
- ☐ Identify your top ten target accounts or stakeholders.
- ☐ Segment your market area, accounts, and stakeholders.
- ☐ Map your buying cycle.
- ☐ Provide visibility and transparency.

PRODUCTIVITY TOOLS

- ■ SWOT Analysis
- ■ Identify and Classify
- ■ Prioritize and Plan Time

To gain access to powerful productivity tools, online learning and courses for acceleration, go to:

www.IgniteYourSellingPotential.com

Clarity + Strategy + Intention + Choice
= Acceleration to Your Destination

TRANSFORM ACTIVITY INTO PRODUCTIVITY®:
APPLY, RELEASE, AND TAKE ACTION

1. What did you learn that you can **apply?**

2. What activity is holding you back from achieving your goals that you can **release?**

3. When can you **take action** to achieve your desired results?

GAIN VISIBILITY AND ACCOUNTABILITY

VISIBILITY + METRICS + ACCOUNTABILITY
= ACCELERATED PERFORMANCE

When things go wrong in your command, start searching for the reason in increasingly large circles around your own desk.

—GEN. BRUCE CLARKE

You can't improve what you don't measure. When an individual or team doesn't hit their goals, oftentimes, they are not measuring the right metrics.

People who know what to measure, why to measure it, and how it should be measured have clear expectations. Together, this helps them focus their effort and resources in the right place to achieve results. Measuring what matters most and having an accountability partner significantly accelerates revenue and results and fuels stronger relationships.

Successful people recognize they can do far more with and through others as opposed to going it alone. The hazard to avoid is falling into the activity trap with the hundreds of e-mails and incoming messages. Commitment and accountability allow people to focus on the things that matter most and to say no to those activities that don't produce results. Focusing on the right metrics will free you from mundane activities and help you ignite your potential, increase your productivity, and achieve your desired results.

By the end of this chapter, you will learn what the top 5 percent do that works and why selecting metrics that matter, an accountability partner, and a practical scorecard are essential to your success. You will also gain insight into which hazards to avoid in order to succeed.

Why are the right metrics so important? Consider the case of a former client of mine as an example. The president of this small, family-owned business called me because he wanted to grow his sales. When I first sat down with him, it was evident he had some significant selling challenges and needed help. The company had a lot of peaks and valleys and very little consistency in their sales. Prior to working with him, the sales team measured things that didn't matter and as a result, didn't achieve their goals. For example, their inside sales team measured the number of proposals completed, and if they completed 20 percent more proposals year over year, they considered that a success.

Now, a higher quantity of activity doesn't necessarily produce productivity. In this case, each proposal cost the company a lot of money because it involved multiple people's time to complete, and their closing ratio was still very low. My recommendation was to change the metric they focused on to the closing ratio.

Instead of spending more resources on the wrong activity, which produced fewer sales, they worked to increase their closing ratio to drive higher sales productivity. We changed the focus to quality not quantity.

We implemented this change—and a few more metrics— and turned the company around in four short months. In fact, it was such a remarkable turnaround that the sales team was able to take a significant amount of business away from the competition. Things went so well that the president invited me to meet with his executive team and help them prepare to sell the company. In six months, we turned around sales and sold the company. The president was very pleased and ended up exceeding his personal and professional goals.

HAZARDS TO AVOID

Common hazards are falling into the activity trap by measuring metrics that don't matter or having too many metrics. Others include the wrong use of metrics, impaired visibility and communication, and lack of accountability. Those who go off-road or spin their wheels may be doing one or more of the above.

How do individuals, teams, and organizations arrive at their destination and achieve their sales goals monthly, quarterly, and annually? They do it one step at a time with the right actions focused on results.

GETTING THE METRICS THAT MATTER MOST

Getting the metrics that matter most is really important. So many sales teams have the wrong metrics. Thus, they achieve the wrong result. That is why metrics are a part of my company name: MR^3, a metrics-driven sales, leadership and productivity consulting firm.

Some sales professionals and teams just measure the final number and not the daily and weekly numbers that lead up to the final number. This sets them up to fail. If you simply measure the end number, you don't have any way to course correct along the way. For anyone to meet or exceed their goal, they need to identify the key activities that lead up to their goal and gain visibility before they arrive there. **Success is made up of daily disciplines and actions that become weekly disciplines and actions.** It's like driving in your car to your destination. Your GPS tells you how far you have traveled and how many miles it will take you to get to your destination.

It's important that you measure the right set of metrics daily, weekly, monthly, and quarterly to help you achieve your goal. Successful sales people and sales teams establish a cadence or rhythm of disciplines whereby each person is consistently enacting the right behaviors to meet or exceed the goals.

The first step is to assess which metrics will drive the right results. To identify the right metrics for the right results we need to understand the two types of metrics. There are **quantitative metrics** and **qualitative metrics.**

Quantitative metrics are measured with facts and numbers. Qualitative metrics are subjective and include assessments based upon behaviors or skill proficiency. Both categories can be further broken down into lagging and leading indicators. Lagging indicators are like looking in the rearview mirror and measuring what has already happened. Leading metrics are future metrics that provide you with visibility on how you are progressing toward your goal and allow you to course correct if necessary. The following table shows an example of each.

You need to focus on both lagging and leading metrics to get the fullest picture. If you use only lagging indicators, then you may spot problems too late, and time may run out before you can do anything about missing your revenue target.

Examples of the difference are as follows:

QUANTITATIVE LAGGING	QUANTITATIVE LEADING
Sales results—after the fact	Sales pipeline revenue dollars per step

One key difference in qualitative metrics is that they are subjective. The focus is not only on the metric but the behavior, such as knowledge, skills, and confidence. It's the art and the science. Looking at leading qualitative metrics allows you to change your course and correct your behavior to reach your goal. For example, if a sales professional has a closing ratio of 75 percent and has demonstrated low confidence, a sales manager can train or coach that individual to improve confidence with selling skills and ultimately increase their closing ratio to achieve their sales goal.

It's beyond the scope of this book to cover the topic of metrics fully. More information on this topic is available in courses.

Below are a couple of examples of qualitative metrics.

QUALITATIVE LAGGING	QUALITATIVE LEADING
Knowledge demonstrated	Knowledge improved

Successful people focus on the behavior habits they need to achieve their desired results.

SELECT AN ACCOUNTABILITY PARTNER

Individuals who have an accountability partner always outperform those who don't. **The accountability partner's role is to challenge you and hold you accountable. It's your role to put forth the effort and pay the price with the hard work required to succeed.** If there is no accountability and no consequence for not showing up or not achieving your goal, then you will be less likely to achieve it. Accountability also gives you the freedom to focus on the priorities that matter most and let go of or say no to the activities that prevent you from achieving your goals. An accountability partner will help you be responsible for your actions and ensure that you are able to explain the value of those actions.

When selecting an accountability partner, choose someone who will not let you off the hook, who will ask you to explain your actions, and who shares your expectations for a successful accountability relationship. Also, set up some consequences and course corrections if you don't follow through. Don't select a friend who will support your justification for not showing up. Sometimes, friends won't be honest with each other, because they fear it will jeopardize the friendship.

TWO-STAGE STRATEGY TO ACHIEVE YOUR DESIRED OUTCOMES

1. REFLECT ON PROGRESS AND COURSE CORRECT

What's working and helping me get to my destination? What do I need to do differently to arrive at my destination on time or early? For example, if you have to make up a 10 percent deficit from last month on top of this month's goals, the question is, "What can I do to achieve 100 percent of my goal for this month + 10 percent from last month?"

2. REWARD

Link exceeding your goal to a reward that is meaningful to you personally and to your team. Some managers don't believe in individual and team rewards. They believe people are rewarded in their paychecks and that's enough, which results in low performance. I disagree with that philosophy. Rewards for above-and-beyond performance provide a vehicle for enhanced focus and motivation. The key is to only reward *above-and-beyond* performance. If your manager doesn't believe in rewards, reward yourself when you exceed your goals by coming up with something meaningful to you.

SUCCESSFUL LEADERS USE METRICS TO IGNITE THE POWER OF PEOPLE

As a manager or leader, you need to make sure your metrics support the following equation: **Value People + Ignite Potential = Achieve Results**

It has to happen in that order. If you are a manager, good performance occurs when you value people as your greatest asset and care about your people in addition to focusing on performance. Metrics don't come first; people do. It's always people first + potential to achieve performance.

> *Metrics don't come first; people do. It's always people first + potential to achieve performance.*

To ignite the selling potential of the team and organization, I recommend that the vice president of sales send sales metric updates to the internal customers and departments that enable or support sales. Include in this a performance summary, best practices, and direction on actionable steps to achieve desired results. Underperforming organizations are, typically, missing these key elements. Including these elements increases the collaboration and leverages the selling potential of the entire organization to develop a laser focus on the internal and external customers.

Making sure the right training is available is also critical to using metrics well and learning how to create visibility and accountability. I often see metrics and dashboards created for an executive team, but they don't deliver value to the sales team and managers. Customer relationship management tools (CRMs) need to include value to the sales team and anyone interacting with the CRM. **Sales compliance increases when value is created.** Entering factual data on a consistent basis is essential to optimizing the client experience.

When leaders hear me talk about metrics, oftentimes, they will run off and quickly establish metrics that strive to achieve results. However, if they don't establish the right metrics and they lack the training and the accountability to back them up, they can take their team off-road and into the ditch. Establishing metrics, gaining visibility, and communicating metrics is an art and a science. It takes experience and proven results to do this well.

BALANCED SCORECARD

As we discussed in Accelerator 3, successful businesses know the key to acceleration and sustainability is a balanced portfolio wheel at the personal level and a balanced scorecard for the business.

> *Establishing metrics, gaining visibility, and communicating metrics is an art and a science. It takes experience and proven results to do this well.*

I recommend using a strategic balanced portfolio wheel to define success so you can make intentional choices in your current professional role as well as your personal life. The aim of the balanced scorecard is to keep track of multiple metrics and behaviors that will enable you to repeat and sustain success, results, and performance. I like to focus on the balanced set of behaviors and metrics. When people ask me what it takes to ignite selling potential and accelerate revenue and achieve results, my answer is always that it's not one thing. Rather, it's a system of activities, metrics, and processes focused on igniting selling potential

> *It's a system of activities, metrics, and processes focused on igniting selling potential and delivering value to people that drives performance.*

and delivering value to people that drives performance. It takes consistent behaviors and disciplines. Success doesn't happen overnight. However, it can be accelerated if you have a roadmap to drive revenue and results fast.

Once you start using this balanced scorecard approach, you will gain the visibility needed to make strategic intentional choices that drive revenue and results at the individual, team, and organizational level. I have found utilizing the balanced scorecard approach a great asset to managing my business and growing revenue.

The balanced scorecard has evolved from its early use as a simple performance measurement framework to a full strategic planning and management system. The "new" balanced scorecard transforms an organization's strategic plan from an attractive but passive document into the "marching orders" for the organization on a daily basis. It provides a framework that not only provides performance measurements but helps planners identify what should be done and measured. It enables executives to truly execute their strategies.

Drs. Robert S. Kaplan and David P. Norton, authors of *The Institute Way: Simplify Strategic Planning and Management with the Balanced Scorecard,* describe the innovation of the balanced scorecard as follows: "The balanced scorecard retains traditional financial measures. But financial measures tell the story of past events, an adequate story for industrial age companies for which investments in long-term capabilities and customer relationships were not critical for success. These financial measures are inadequate, however, for guiding and evaluating the journey that information age companies must make to create future value through investment in customers, suppliers, employees, processes, technology, and innovation."

Defining success for a team often comes in the form of a strategic plan. When I lead individuals and executive teams through strategic planning, it's so gratifying when they tell me how much it means to them to have clarity and know that their role and contribution makes a difference in achieving results, accelerating revenue, and delivering value to the clients, team, and company. They walk away feeling inspired and motivated. Once again, it's all about people and treating them as your greatest asset and then, igniting their potential to achieve results. Successful leaders give their people what they need to succeed. When you gain clarity and define in writing what success is both personally and professionally, you will recognize the difference you make! Do it now. Don't wait.

COMMUNICATION OF METRICS IS KEY—ABOVE, BELOW, ACROSS

Everyone needs consistent feedback on how they're progressing because it provides fuel and inspiration as well as guidance about whether to continue on the current path or make changes. When it comes to sales, successful top performers keep score and know their sales metrics to course correct as needed to exceed their goal. I call this sales analytics. Ideally, the sales manager sends these out to all sales reps with recognition of those who have exceeded their goal and any direction or guidance on what is needed for the rest of the team to exceed their goal.

Managers who successfully drive performance and help their people ignite and maximize their potential to accelerate revenue and achieve results hold their teams accountable. This increases their sphere of influence and followership. **Building a culture of accountability, teamwork, and winning fuels strong, healthy relationships.** Some of my best relationships and friendships of 20+ years were developed when I was either on a winning team or leading a winning team. If you are manager and are not focused on building teamwork, accountability, and winning, start now. Why? It's essential to job satisfaction and the people on your team.

> *Measuring what matters most is essential to success.*

ACCELERATOR 6 ACTION ITEMS

CHECKLIST: STRATEGIES FOR ACCELERATION

☐ Identify the metrics that matter.

☐ Gain visibility on your progress.

☐ Select an accountability partner.

☐ Communicate progress to goals.

☐ Reflect, revise, and refocus as needed to achieve goals.

PRODUCTIVITY TOOLS

■ My Strategic 1-on-1 Scorecard

To gain access to powerful productivity tools, online learning and courses for acceleration, go to:

www.IgniteYourSellingPotential.com

Clarity + Strategy + Intention + Choice
= Acceleration to Your Destination

TRANSFORM ACTIVITY INTO PRODUCTIVITY®: APPLY, RELEASE, AND TAKE ACTION

1. What did you learn that you can **apply?**

2. What activity is holding you back from achieving your goals that you can **release?**

3. When can you **take action** to achieve your desired results?

CREATE VALUE AND DIFFERENTIATION

VALUE + DIFFERENTIATION = CHOICE

Try not to become men of success.
Rather, become men of value.

—**ALBERT EINSTEIN**

No matter what you are selling, you have to consistently create value and differentiation to empower your customers to choose your products and services.

The more buy-in you gain, the more value you can deliver, and the faster you can succeed. If you are trying to earn business away from the competition, you must focus on synchronizing your communication with the choices your customers make to make it easy for your customers to choose you instead of the competition.

People get frustrated when the customer doesn't see value in their product, service, idea, or solution. The reality is that so many people enter into interactions, discussions, and meetings with no preparation, plan, or focus on how to do this well. As a result, they have unproductive conversations and meetings that waste time. They walk away with little to no buy-in or next steps. In this chapter you will learn how not to fall into that trap but instead, create value during every interaction so your customers choose you instead of the competition.

THE DIFFERENCE IS YOU

The good news is *you* are in the driver's seat and by synchronizing the way you communicate with the choices your customers make, you will be able to create a repeatable, consistent customer experience that earns trust and generates revenue and results. If you are a leader communicating with your team members, you will be able to gain followership and buy-in from your team. The key to all successful communication is to focus on the person you are communicating to. That means tailoring your message to be synchronized with how they receive and use information.

> *Selling is about empowering your customers to make good choices to solve their unmet needs and overcome their challenges.*

Selling is about empowering your customers to make good choices to solve their unmet needs and overcome their challenges. The fun of selling is creating value and helping people overcome their challenges and succeed. However, it's important to recognize the value exchange. To succeed, you need a compelling and unique value proposition or a CVP for short.

CREATING VALUE AND DIFFERENTIATION

Unmet Need + Compelling Unique Value (CVP) + ROI =
Accelerated Revenue, Results,
and Stronger Relationships

A CVP is a compelling and unique value proposition. People don't buy features; they buy solutions to their problems. Value is not just in the product, service, or solution but in how well a sales professional understands the client's needs and then communicates and differentiates how well they can help the client meet those needs.

To create a CVP, I suggest you map out the unmet needs you solve best with your product, service, or solution. To make it easy for you, I have mapped it out visually in the following example. You want to identify the unmet needs you solve well to add value to your customers. You also want to identify the top three strengths of your product, service, or solution, which are called the features. A feature describes a strength that comes from what your product is or how it works. Outline the benefit of solving those needs relative to your top three strengths.

Let's review an example using the iPhone 6 and 6 Plus.

UNMET NEEDS: PROBLEMS OR CHALLENGES LIST THE TOP 3-5 PROBLEMS YOU SOLVE	FEATURE: UNIQUE STRENGTH, WHAT OR HOW IT WORKS	BENEFIT: ADVANTAGE OR GAIN FOR THE CUSTOMER
Greater visibility	**Larger Screen:** The iPhone 6 and 6 Plus screens are 4.7 inches and 5.5 inches, matching the screen sizes of rival smartphones.	Enhanced visibility and surface area for ease of use
Minimize breakage	**Durable Screen:** New iPhone screens have "ion-strengthened" glass.	Breakage is less likely than before.
Clear, sharp pictures	8 megapixels on camera	Photos are now noticeably sharper, with faster, more precise autofocus and better sensors.
Ease of use and **easy to sync with apple devices and cloud**	Synchronizes with the apple devices and cloud	**No hassles with automatic synchronization**
Be able to count on a longer battery life.	**Longer battery life**	You can count on batteries. iPhone 6 will last 25 percent longer on 3G browsing than the iPhone 5S, and the iPhone 6 Plus will last even longer.

Value is created when you uncover the unmet needs and problems that your products, services, or solutions solve and then link that benefit back to the customer. Differentiated value is further created by knowing the competition and differentiating your brand, yourself, your company, and your solution from the competition, and the return is greater than the cost. That's why ROI is essential.

UNDERSTANDING THE DELTA

The delta is the difference between what you are offering and what your customer is currently using, doing, or considering purchasing. Every now and then, I hear someone say, "I don't have any competition." If someone is selling a new technology or service, they may feel like they don't have any direct competitors. In such cases, however, the competition is the status quo. If a customer has to change their workflow or stop doing something and start doing something new to use your product or service, there is a cost of switching. An example of this would be a CRM or customer relationship management system. CRMs cross over into many functions beyond sales. Someone who sells CRMs into companies may need to get buy-in from IT, sales, operations, and the management team. While one group may buy in, others may not see the value in making the switch. The value has to be greater than the cost.

UNMET NEED + FEATURE + BENEFIT
AND ROI = VALUE PROPOSITION

You can reduce your objections and increase your sales by a minimum of 10 percent by preparing, planning, and focusing on discovering unmet needs and delivering differentiated value with this process to help your customers succeed. While you never want to say anything negative about the competition, you do want to differentiate and create a delta. Here is an example using the iPhone 6 once again:

UNMET NEED: MINIMIZE BREAKAGE

Unmet Need: You mentioned it was important to have a screen that wouldn't break if dropped.

Unique Feature: The new iPhone 6 has a durable screen with ion-strengthened glass.

Benefit/Advantage: It's less likely to break if dropped than the phone you have.

Questions to ask yourself:

1. What unmet needs do you satisfy? What problems do you solve?

2. Who has these problems? Which companies have these problems? Which customers need what you do?

3. Who is your ideal customer? That may include the most profitable customers and strategic influencers.

4. Based upon the problems you solve, what is your unique differentiator?

UNMET NEED/ PROBLEM	FEATURE	ADVANTAGE

PROBLEM/ UNMET NEEDS YOU SOLVE	FEATURES	ADVANTAGE
the iPhone	Operating System	Ease of use; Integration across devices; Cloud integration; Easy synching and integration

When you go to purchase a phone, many times the salesperson wants to tell you everything about it—even things you're not interested in. Gaining buy-in is all about understanding the customer's needs, linking the features and benefits of your product to the customer's needs, and creating the differentiated value exchange. Customers don't care about a bunch of features and benefits that don't address their needs or challenges. The value exchange is the price the customers pay in exchange for the value you provide and the delta or the difference between the competition or status quo.

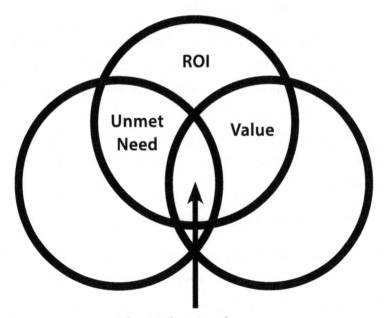

The Value Exchange

HAZARDS TO AVOID

Failing to prepare, plan, and focus is very common and easily avoidable. As you focus on external customers, don't neglect internal stakeholders and direct reports because it will cause them to move away instead of toward you. Steer clear of focusing on yourself instead of the internal customer. If managers neglect the needs of their internal customers and direct reports, they may experience low morale, attrition, lack of buy-in, or an unproductive team.

Individuals, teams, and organizations run into challenges when they try to be all things to all customers. Stay focused on your ideal customers and delivering differentiated value during every interaction. That's how you, your team, and your organization will be successful.

SEVEN STEPS TO MAKE IT EASY FOR YOUR CUSTOMERS TO BUY

Selling is planned communication to identify needs and gain agreement on a mutually beneficial exchange of value. Value plus differentiation means the value of buying needs to be greater than the price of not buying. Planned communication is far more effective when you use this simple equation, which will make it easy for your customers to choose you instead of the competition or status quo.

Purpose + Plan + Process = Productive Communication

The following seven-step process will help you accelerate your revenue, achieve results, and deliver differentiated value to your customers.

STEP 1: PRECALL PLANNING

Before you do anything else, create an agenda with a purpose, payoff, and plan for your customer interaction, whether it will be via phone or a face-to-face meeting. Without this precall planning, gaining access can be challenging. Many sales professionals have a hard time getting customers to call them back to schedule a meeting or a phone call. Oftentimes, it's because their communication, whether via voicemail or e-mail, lacks an agenda with a purpose to deliver value for the customer.

When you do finally meet with a customer and don't gain buy-in, the question is, "What did your agenda consist of?" If you don't have an agenda, it can be challenging to get attendance.

STEP 2: BUILD RAPPORT, CONNECT, AND CARE

Your customer will be choosing whether or not to buy from you based on how you show up. What research have you done on the company and person? What questions can you ask to connect and get to know the person? **You demonstrate you care by coming prepared. Care about your customer and focus on helping them succeed.** So many sales people lead with pushing their product, service or solution but that's not a formula for success.

STEP 3: ASK, LISTEN, LEARN, AND AGREE

Asking and listening is essential to discovering unmet needs. Successful people do the following:

Good sales people ask great questions. There are different categories of questions you need to ask to know how to navigate through the conversation effectively and efficiently. (See examples of questions outlined in this chapter.) Once you've asked the questions, you should spend the majority of the conversation listening to your customer's answers. People who influence others and gain buy-in understand the importance of listening. **Listening builds trust and relationships. It makes the other person feel valued.** Making others feel valued is important to helping them succeed. We have two ears and one mouth because we were designed to listen more than talk! Listening is an active process and a skill. One way to listen effectively and capture what's important to the other person is to take notes.

Good sales people think of the conversation as a discovery process rather than an opportunity to push their product, service or solution. The key is to guide the conversation with a proven, repeatable process so your customers can discover the needs you, your company, and your solution solve. Thinking of the conversation as a discovery process is important for two reasons. First, customers don't always know their needs. When you go to buy something, do you always know exactly what you need? For example, when I purchased a new laptop, the technology had advanced so much from the time I purchased my previous laptop that it was difficult to figure out what type of computer best met my needs. It was only after several sales professionals asked me a number of questions that I was able to figure it out. The same applies to your solutions to your customer's problems. When selling, successful people ask focused and productive questions targeted toward uncovering the needs they solve for their customer. If you ask general, unfocused questions, you may uncover needs your competition solves but not needs you solve that differentiate your company and solution.

Second, research shows that your customer is only likely to remember 10 percent of what you say, so leading by talking about your product, service or solution is probably not going to be very effective. However, if they discover for themselves through your conversation what is beneficial about your solution, the rate of retention increases to 90 percent! This is why it's so important to make the conversation a discovery process. I view selling as educating with a purpose, using a facilitative approach that allows the customer to be in the driver's seat. That way they can discover, learn, and take ownership for solving their own problems. This empowers them and sets them up for success.

Good sales people show the customer they've heard them by acknowledging what they've said and summarizing what they understand is important to the customer. It's important to gain agreement that your understanding captures what's important to them before moving on. After customers have listened to you summarizing their needs, ask a check-in question such as, "Did I capture everything that's important to you?" That gives them an opportunity to agree, correct, or add to what you have summarized.

Seeking agreement on what's important is a critical step prior to creating value. This is not about the transaction. Selling is a people and performance business. Successful people who ignite their selling potential focus first on helping the customer succeed personally and professionally and create value for their customer during every interaction. The key is that you don't go into presentation mode until you have established the unmet needs you can solve and the customer agrees they have unmet needs they want to be solved.

WHAT DOES THE EVIDENCE SAY?

Telling has a 5 percent retention rate! Teaching and engaging your customer in a participatory conversation has a 90 percent retention rate.

THE LEARNING PYRAMID

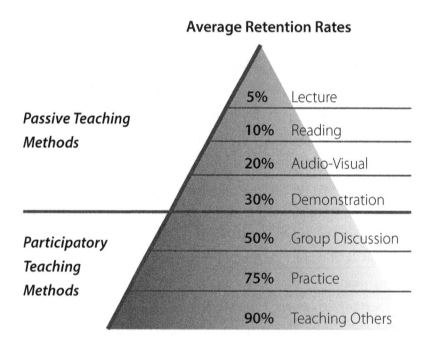

Average Retention Rates

Passive Teaching Methods
- 5% Lecture
- 10% Reading
- 20% Audio-Visual
- 30% Demonstration

Participatory Teaching Methods
- 50% Group Discussion
- 75% Practice
- 90% Teaching Others

Adapted from National Training Laboratories in Bethel, Maine.

NOBODY WANTS TO BE SOLD, BUT EVERYONE LIKES TO BUY!

That is why it's so important to ask, listen, learn, and let your customers buy. The ratio I like to use is this: You should spend about 10 percent of the conversation talking, mostly asking questions, and 90 percent of the conversation listening to your customers. **Let your customers participate. Empower them!**

STEP 4. DIFFERENTIATE YOUR COMPANY, DIVISION, AND DEPARTMENT

One of the questions you should be asking in Step 3 is "What do you look for in a partner and company?" Based on the answer to that question, you can present your capabilities, culture match, and case studies of like customers who have benefited from your solutions, services, or products. Making clear how these things meet their needs is how you differentiate yourself.

Keep in mind, however, that if you find out early in your questioning process that this is not an ideal client, then you don't need to continue with this step. As we learned in Accelerator 2, there is no reason to chase after nonideal customers who are not a good match.

STEP 5. PRESENT YOUR SOLUTION, PRODUCT, IDEA, OR CONCEPT

This is where you take the unmet needs your customer agreed they have and present your solution. Value is created when you link your differentiated solution to the customer's unmet needs.

STEP 6. PRESENT THE RETURN ON INVESTMENT

Use of an ROI may also be referred to as economic selling. When I used to manage a nationwide marketing team, we did a lot of economic selling to executive teams. This is typically an area where the people selling need skill development to do this well. Value exchange is when the customer recognizes what they are getting in exchange for their payment and the value is in their favor. In other words, the customer sees that the value they will receive from the investment they are making is worth more to their business than the cost.

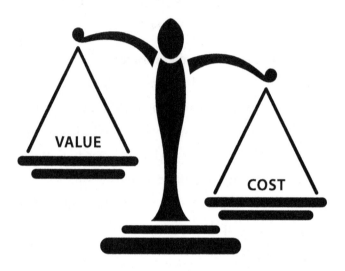

When you are gaining agreement to purchase, there needs to be a greater return on investment for the customer to make the purchase worthwhile. For example, if they are going to switch from a competitor, there is a switching cost. How are you going to provide greater value than the cost of switching or converting to your company and solution?

Successful people ask questions up front to quantify needs and then produce a meaningful, relevant return on investment. Following is an example.

EXAMPLE OF PROVIDING A MEANINGFUL ROI

I worked with a company whose business revolved around improving content management and workflow processes. Accessing content on a company's intranet can be a huge challenge, as content stored electronically grows at a rapid pace every day. This company offered the ability to categorize that content so it could be easily accessed by employees around the globe.

Quantifying questions that sales professionals at this company could ask clients include:

- How many clicks does it take to find content on your intranet?
- How much does it cost you per employee if they have to click five times to locate a document?
- How many employees need to access that information?

How much does that equate to in $ per minutes of wasted time multiplied by the number of employees worldwide?

Based on the answers to those questions, a meaningful ROI could be calculated this way:

10,000 employees x 1 hour of wasted time each day trying to find content for sales presentations and proposals.

At $50/hour per employee x 10,000 employees = $500,000 is wasted each day searching for content.

If the solution the company was offering cost $100,000, then the customer's ROI would be 5:1 in one day!

STEP 7. AGREE TO REFER, BUY AGAIN, OR NEXT STEPS

This is when the customer agrees to choose you, your company, and your solution instead of the competition, which can also be the status quo. Remember, everyone is selling, unselling, or being outsold every day. So if you are a manager within a company and you are trying to gain buy-in for your ideas, you can also benefit by learning how to create differentiated value.

Be sure to follow up after your meeting. Sales communication includes precall planning and postcall follow-up. If you don't follow up, you are actually unselling. This is a common mistake low performers make. The good news is that you can change that by following up within 48 hours of your meeting. This is equally important for companies that have services to implement or install.

The customer may buy into the solution, but if the implementation or installation is not executed well, the customer may not buy again. **Be sure your service team is delivering value during every interaction, along with your sales team.**

NAVIGATING AROUND CHALLENGES

By following the seven-step process I just outlined, you will make it easy for your customers to buy from you. There are, however, some common pitfalls that can steer people off course. Following is some guidance on how to navigate those pitfalls to achieve success.

CHALLENGE #1: TROUBLE GAINING ACCESS OR BUY-IN

Access continues to be a growing challenge, especially because of the pace at which the marketplace and businesses are moving today. With the average person sending and receiving 125+ communications (e-mails, instant messages, and texts) a day and companies asking their employees to do more with less, many potential clients are simply overwhelmed and distracted. In addition, customers are able to access a lot of information on the Internet to make purchasing decisions, which means there is less reliance on sales professionals for education. Together, this means that it can be very hard to gain access to a potential customer and to get them to spend their valuable time listening to you. The same holds true for internal stakeholders. If you don't quickly give people a reason to meet with you, let them know what's in it for them, and let them know how much time you will need from them, then why should they give you their time?

What to do: In any interaction with a customer, you want to be sure to open by listing the outcomes so your meeting is focused on delivering value to the customer. This is starting with the end in mind. Then, you can plan your conversation to achieve that outcome. It's also important to gain agreement on the outcomes by asking the customer what they want to walk away with from your time together. This is really important and allows you to tailor your time together to meet their objectives and deliver value to them. You can do this by simply asking, "What do you want to walk away with from our time together?"

You can use the same principle in a voicemail or e-mail requesting a meeting to help ensure that you gain the access you're looking for. Following is an example of how to construct an e-mail that will help you gain access:

Start with a compelling purpose telling the customer why you are asking for their time. Also, make clear how much of their time you are asking for: "The purpose of this message is to request 30 minutes of your time to get to know you, learn about your priorities and challenges, and XYZ company's capabilities to determine if I can be of service to you."

Next, list the topics you want to discuss and learn more about. This lets the customer know where you are going in the conversation to achieve your shared outcomes: "Customers choose (XYZ staffing) services when they want to overcome their staffing challenges." *State the needs you solve.*

Next, list the quantifiable benefits clients have experienced using your services:

- saved 15 percent in labor costs

- reduced downtime of an open position from three months to one month

- upgraded role two grades from a VP level director

Close with a promise from you: "I will come prepared to maximize our time together. Please let me know what dates and times work best in the next two weeks. [*Be specific and list a timeframe.*] Let me know if you want me to work with someone to get on your schedule."

Best regards,

[Your name]

TURN IDEAS INTO ACTION

1. **If you don't have time to plan a meeting so it delivers value to your internal or external customers, why should they take time to meet with you?** What percentage of your time do you spend preparing and

planning before a meeting with your internal and external customers?

2. What percentage of your time do you spend on follow-up after a meeting or call? How many times have you left a meeting wondering what the next step was?

3. Many professionals spend 90 percent of their time in meetings and 10 percent of their remaining time trying to catch up on e-mails and work. That leaves 0 percent of their time for precall planning and 0 percent for proactive postcall follow-up. How productive do you think those meetings are? **What percentage of your time do you spend in conversations or meetings that have no purpose, outcomes, or follow-up? What a waste of time.**

High-performing individuals, teams, and organizations spend 65–80 percent of their time proactively doing precall or premeeting preparation, call strategy, and planning by beginning with the end in mind. What can you do to shift your priorities to spend more time on what matters most?

CHALLENGE #2: TROUBLE STEERING THE CONVERSATION

The right questions will help you discover what unmet needs to focus on solving and what you need to do to empower your customer and help them succeed. Questions are a discovery tool. Great questions transform how we think. They

> *Great questions transform how we think.*

will help you and your customers discover their unmet needs, which they may not have otherwise discovered on their own.

Questioning is a tool, and like with any tool, the key is in how it's used. You should ask questions with a pure and positive intent to help customers succeed. That is how I advocate using questions. However, some individuals misuse questions. They use questions to manipulate or turn up the heat or interrogate the customer. This is a self-serving, negative use of questions that is to be avoided. It's important with this tool, or any other tool, to use it for a positive purpose to help people succeed.

Following are questions you can ask, divided into categories that, collectively, will give you an understanding of what the person's needs are, how they buy, and more importantly, how to navigate through the conversation to create differentiated value and gain agreement on next steps.

QUESTIONS ABOUT THE CUSTOMER

These questions are designed to help you know how to navigate the landscape you are in. It's tough to do this if you don't understand the particulars of the landscape. Depending upon what you're selling, there can be more than one person involved in making the decision. More and more decisions are made in teams. Even if you have one or two people making the decision, there can be more people influencing the decision when it comes to installing or implementing the solution.

For example, in consumer and retail sales, you have a buyer at the corporate headquarters or a buying team. To drive sales, you may have to work through the store managers. To gain strong pull-through, you may need to gain buy-in from the regional or zone managers whom the store managers report to.

Another example is in health care. While you may be selling to the physician, hospitals have set up committees and purchasing teams to consolidate costs. The days of selling directly to doctors are diminishing. These buying committees are trying to reduce the physician preference in order to standardize and negotiate better pricing. You may need to gain buy-in from the entire committee.

Regardless of what you're selling, it's important to know the landscape. For all the reasons mentioned above as well as the fact that your primary contact could leave and go to another organization, it's important to develop relationships with more than one person. Always establish a primary and secondary champion within the account. Questions may include:

Person

- What is your role and responsibility here at your company?

- What is your background?

Organization

- Structure: How is your organization structured?

- Understand reporting structure: Whom do you report to?

- Priorities: What are your organization's top three strategic priorities in the next 6–12 months?

- What are your top three priorities in the next 6–12 months?

- Culture: How would you describe your culture?

- Competitive advantage: How does your company differentiate itself from the competition?

QUESTIONS ABOUT DIFFERENTIATED NEEDS, CHALLENGES, AND SUCCESS

It's important to use questions to uncover the unmet needs of the customer so you can help them solve them. As you ask these questions, think about aiming for the center of a target. If you ask questions that are unfocused or away from the center of the target, which are not differentiated needs you solve, you are wasting your customer's time. You need to uncover their unmet needs and find out what success looks like for them so you can help them achieve success.

- What challenges do you anticipate in achieving your top priorities?

- What has been your experience in overcoming those challenges?

- What does success look like for you personally?

- What does success look like for your organization?

- Competition: What other alternatives, if any, are you exploring?

- Budget: What budget dollars are allocated to address these challenges?

- Timing: What is your timeline to address those challenges?

QUESTIONS ABOUT THE DECISION-MAKING PROCESS

To come to an agreement, there are specific things you need to know about how this person and organization make their decisions.

- What is your decision-making process?

- Who besides yourself influences the decision?

- Who will be the advocates? Who are the advisories?

- Who has autonomy to make the final decision?

KNOWING HOW TO ASK OPEN-ENDED QUESTIONS

Asking great questions helps your customer discover differentiated, unmet needs that you can solve. The questions above will help you ask the focused questions to uncover unmet needs you solve better than your competition. Let's not tell. Instead, let your customers buy. The questions above will help you understand what to focus on to deliver value to your customers and earn the right to advance to the next step.

As you do this, an important thing to keep in mind is that you want to use open-ended questions instead of closed-ended ones. Closed-ended questions can be answered with a yes or no and are used to gain agreement, whereas open-ended questions help you understand your customer's needs and empower your customer. Open-ended questions are those that begin with

- Who

- What

- Where

- How

- Why

IN SUMMARY

Selling is not telling, rather it's about making it easy for your customers to buy. The difference is you—in how you help your

> *Selling is not telling, rather it's about making it easy for your customers to buy.*

customer discover their unmet needs, how your solution solves those needs, and the differentiated value you provide. This is what will help them choose you instead of the competition.

Prepare, plan, and focus on delivering differentiated value during every interaction. Follow up, follow up, follow up after every conversation with your customer.

ACCELERATOR 7 ACTION ITEMS

CHECKLIST: STRATEGIES FOR ACCELERATION

☐ Map out your features with the greatest strengths, the benefits to your customer, and the unmet needs you solve, as a company, and with your solution.

☐ List your competitive advantages for each feature or strength.

☐ Build a question list to uncover the unmet needs you solve.

☐ Create and quantify the return on investment (ROI) a customer can expect.

☐ Prepare, plan, and focus sales conversations on discovering unmet needs and delivering differentiated value to your customers during every interaction.

PRODUCTIVITY TOOLS

■ Value Proposition

To gain access to powerful productivity tools, online learning and courses for acceleration, go to:

www.IgniteYourSellingPotential.com

Clarity + Strategy + Intention + Choice
= Acceleration to Your Destination

TRANSFORM ACTIVITY INTO PRODUCTIVITY®:
APPLY, RELEASE, AND TAKE ACTION

1. What did you learn that you can **apply?**

2. What activity is holding you back from achieving your goals that you can **release?**

3. When can you **take action** to achieve your desired results?

DRIVERS START YOUR ENGINES

Congratulations on completing this book! You have taken the first step to accelerating revenue, achieving results, and fueling stronger relationships. As you continue to apply what you learned, you will experience greater personal and job satisfaction. You will also be prepared to navigate around your challenges to your desired destination and gain a competitive advantage.

HOW CAN YOU ACCELERATE?

ROADMAP FOR INDIVIDUAL, TEAM, AND ORGANIZATION ACCELERATION

STEP 1: WANT TO GO IT ALONE?

- Take online assessment to know your score, chart your course, and read book for **self-directed learning.**

- Assessment to know your score can be found at www.IgniteYourSellingPotential.com by clicking on the What's Your Score? button.

WHAT'S YOUR SCORE?
MY SELLING POTENTIAL

- **Application**: Review assessment and chart your course week one. Read one chapter and answer the questions each week for seven weeks as an individual or as a team to achieve results.

STEP 2: WANT NAVIGATION FOR APPLICATION? NEED ACCOUNTABILITY?

- **Enroll in a team-navigated eight-week course, "Application and Accountability."** This is an excellent option for any individual or team.

- **Application**: Take online assessment to chart your course, read book, and join a navigated teleseminar weekly for application and accountability.

STEP 3: WANT FASTER RESULTS? WANT SUSTAINABILITY?

Team Acceleration and Navigation; Gain access to powerful productivity tools + online learning + team navigation.

- **Enroll in a 90-Day Accelerator™ Course "Team Acceleration and Navigation"** with application, accountability, and sustainability. Gain access to powerful tools to gain acceleration to your desired destination.

- **Application:** Take online assessment to chart your course, read book, gain access to online learning with powerful tools, and join a team-navigated teleseminar for weekly application, accountability, and sustainability.

STEP 4: IGNITE YOUR TEAM'S SELLING POTENTIAL

- **Engage Susan A. Lund to speak** at your company meeting. **Get everyone on the same page** with a **common road to revenue and results.**

- **Engage Susan for a full day or half-day workshop** to **navigate around your challenges and achieve results.**

- **Schedule a lunch and learn** with Susan **to inspire, equip, and empower your team!**

STEP 5: BECOME A CERTIFIED SELLING POTENTIAL IGNITER WITHIN YOUR ORGANIZATION.

- Complete a team-navigated 90-Day Accelerator™ Course.

- **Contact us at: contactMR3@MR3Consulting.com** to schedule a call to discuss the qualification criteria and process to transition from a successful individual contributor to a successful igniter within your organization.

- Enroll in our **"Success to Significance Course"** to become certified and make a difference in the lives of others and in your organization.

ADDED TO ANY OF THE ABOVE FOR
FASTER RESULTS AND SUSTAINABILITY:

- Customized workshops tailored precisely to your needs.
- Coaching for results.

These courses are relevant for even the most tenured successful sales executives, sales managers, and senior executives. They are designed to deliver value to each and every participant, team, and organization. All content has been proven and road tested and has been successful within Fortune 500, midsized, and privately held organizations.

For access to assessment and courses go to
www.IgniteYourSellingPotential.com
or call us at 800-281-6084.

Susan A. Lund is the president of MR³, a metrics-driven sales, leadership, and productivity consulting firm in Minnetonka, Minnesota. Susan has more than 30 years of experience in business, sales, sales leadership, sales coaching, sales training, productivity, and executive coaching. During this time, Susan hired, motivated, coached, trained, and led a sales team from $5.2M in sales to $139M in sales in less than three years, scaled sales in multiple organizations, and developed winning teams. As a result, she earned numerous awards for exceeding performance goals.

She has hired, trained, coached, and motivated more than 3,000 senior executives, sales and marketing executives, managers, and sales representatives. Susan has directly managed 120+ people with domestic and international responsibility in sales, marketing, and education. Since founding MR³, she has positively impacted thousands of people and multiple organizations to gain incremental revenue growth. Susan is a sales, leadership, and productivity expert. For access to services with MR³, client results, and upcoming events, go to: **www.MR3Consulting.com**.

How can you use this book?

INSPIRE

EMPOWER

EQUIP

EDUCATE

MOTIVATE

THANK

TRANSFORM

Why have a custom version of *Ignite Your Selling Potential?*

- Build personal bonds with customers, prospects, employees, donors, and key constituencies

- Develop a long-lasting reminder of your event, milestone, or celebration

- Provide a keepsake that inspires change in behavior and change in lives

- Deliver the ultimate "thank you" gift that remains on coffee tables and bookshelves

- Generate the "wow" factor

Books are thoughtful gifts that provide a genuine sentiment that other promotional items cannot express. They promote employee discussions and interaction, reinforce an event's meaning or location, and they make a lasting impression. Use your book to say "Thank You" and show people that you care.

Ignite Your Selling Potential is available in bulk quantities and in customized versions at special discounts for corporate, institutional, and educational purposes. To learn more please contact our Special Sales team at:

1.800.281.6084 • contactMR3@MR3Consulting.com • www.MR3Consulting.com